TWICE THE LUCK

T0208704

TWICE THE LUCK

By: Loren J. "Bart" Bartels

iUniverse, Inc.
New York Bloomington

Twice The Luck
A Diary Of A Minnesota Moose Hunt

iUniverse books may be ordered through booksellers or by contacting:

iUniverse
1663 Liberty Drive
Bloomington, IN 47403
www.iuniverse.com
1-800-Authors (1-800-288-4677)

Because of the dynamic nature of the Internet, any Web addresses or links contained in this book may have changed since publication and may no longer be valid. The views expressed in this work are solely those of the author and do not necessarily reflect the views of the publisher, and the publisher hereby disclaims any responsibility for them.

ISBN: 978-1-4401-3672-6 (pbk)
ISBN: 978-1-4401-3673-3 (ebk)

Printed in the United States of America

iUniverse rev. date: 7/16/2009

The day by day diary of a Minnesota moose hunt

Preface

This book was written for all the hunters who faithfully apply every time the State of Minnesota makes licenses available but, are not successful in obtaining a moose license. For those who are successful, it is a guide as to items they will need, what to expect during the hunt, and the situations they will be confronted with. Also, for the scenic beauty others are seeking in their vacation plans.

May you enjoy your life to the fullest!

That Man Is A Success

Who has lived well,
Laughed often and loved much;

Who has gained the respect
Of intelligent men
And the love of children;

Who has filled the niche
And accomplished his task;

Who leaves the world better
Than he found it,
Whether by an improved poppy,
A perfect poem
Or a rescued soul;

Who never lacked appreciation
Of earths beauty
Or failed to express it;

Who looked for the best in others
And gave the best he had.

Unknown author

Acknowledgements

I acknowledge with deep appreciation, the support and encouragement that I received in various ways from the following:

The Culp family…Encouragement
Terry Mejdrich, Author…Guidance
Sandy and Richard Stefanoc…Typing
Tom Chapin…Corrections
Donna and Pete Nelson…Proof Reading
Benjamin and Tammy O'Brien, friends…Editing
Becky and Jim Jennings……Proofreading
And my close circle of friends at Moose Lodge #2023, Grand Rapids, Minnesota…Constructive criticism and phrasing

About the Author

The author moved from North Dakota to Northern Minnesota with his family at age four. The older boys would let him tag along to carry their game...there he became interested in wildlife and hunting.

He acquired his first firearm, a single shot twenty-two at age nine and became a crack shot. He shot his first deer (a doe) at age eleven, his first buck (a ten pointer) at age thirteen. This started his lifetime of hunting.

While living next to the Mississippi River, he also acquired a keen interest in fishing.

After marriage in 1954, he moved to Grand Marais, Minnesota. While there he learned carpentry and various forms of construction which became his trade. After following construction booms for six years, he eventually settled in the northern suburbs of Minneapolis to raise his five children; however, he and his family kept in close contact with the Grand Marais area.

Lake Superior, the north shore, and the Gunflint Trail presented many challenges for survival. Lake Superior nearly claimed his life on three different occasions while wild animals challenged him on seven different encounters...moose on three, black bear on two, deer on one, and timber wolves on one.

He is now retired and living on his forty acres of wilderness southwest of Hill City, Minnesota.

Loren James Bartels

**We welcome you to ride along and join us on this exciting
adventure in pursuit of Marty, the elusive moose.**

Thursday September 26, 2002

It is one of those beautiful fall afternoons in late September. The air is fresh and clear, and the aspen are starting to get their fall colors. The sky is blue, with pillow-like white clouds floating lazily over the St. Louis River. They look as if they are marking the many multi-colored islands which guide the river as it flows into the crystal clear waters of the great Lake Superior.

From the wayside rest on top of Spirit Mountain, one can view the ski lifts and many trails on the slopes. The hills will soon be bustling with skiers with the first heavy snowfall that will herald the opening of this winter wonderland. We proceed down to the docks of Duluth, the gigantic North American hub for loading and unloading of goods and cargo to be distributed throughout the world. Some huge ocean-going freighters are loading their cargos, and others are hurriedly unloading cubes of various merchandise for mid-west distribution. Soon they will be reloaded for return shipment to other world ports.

Farther ahead are the two high bridges that connect the twin ports of Duluth, Minnesota and Superior, Wisconsin. Wisconsin's shores are clearly in sight and are also gaining their beautiful fall colors. Out on the open water, seven ocean-going ships are in full view at various distances from the harbor. Trails of ripples are flowing behind them, leaving long straight lines on the calm water. This is like being in another world; every direction is a new experience, a new change, a different way of life.

As we look down below us, the maze of highways and concrete overpasses are impressive as they serve to regulate the heavy flow of traffic during rush hour. This maze is also the west end of the famous North Shore Drive with its awesome scenic beauty. Those who have seen the charm of Vermont and the eastern seaboard, along with that of Tennessee, Kentucky and the Smokey Mountains, maintain the North Shore to be equal to, or more exciting than any of them. Very few have ever witnessed the entire season of the North Shore as it changes to its full dress of colors, but many have traveled thousands of miles just to spend one or two days witnessing Superior's North Shore in its full splendor. The many rivers that flow down through rocky gorges and crevices carved out through eons of time pass under the bridges to empty their oxygen-rich waters into Lake Superior. This huge, deep body of water contains one-third of the world's clean fresh water.

As we enter Duluth, a city of modern architecture intermingled with ancient shipping culture, our eyes dance with excitement. From the concrete maze of highways high in the air we have an astonishing view of the waterfront loading docks and large manufacturing plants. To the left, we can see in the distance the Enger Tower standing majestically on top of the Skyline Drive. This has been a famous Duluth landmark since it was built as a lookout over a century ago. A few more miles of new four lane high-

way and we enter an area of artistically decorative tunnels as we pass on the backside of antique buildings that have withstood the elements of time since the sea merchants settled in the early days.

Emerging on Lemon Drop hill, a check point along the route of the famous Grandma's Marathon, we drive through a few more miles of residential variety of renovated dwellings, new homes and huge old mansions, and then a couple miles more to Lester River and we are once

again on the shore of Lake Superior. We soon leave the shoreline and decide to take the expressway to Two Harbors. I then have time to relax and let my mind wander back to the circumstances and good fortune that has brought me here again.

THE FIRST OPPORTUNITY IN 1988

In 1988, I was lead hunter in a party of four, consisting of myself, my hunting buddy Rod, and the O'Connor brothers (Don and Doug). We were lucky enough to be drawn for a Minnesota moose license. At that time the Northeast and Northwest zones of Minnesota were both open, and between the two zones just over 400 licenses were issued by a lottery drawing. The zones are opened and closed as the moose population fluctuates, and are only open every other year if the population allows. 1988 was the last year you could receive a license and still be allowed to apply in four years. It is now a once in a lifetime license; if your name is drawn, you can never apply again, even if for some reason you can't go or don't even see a moose. That's just tough luck. There were over twenty-five thousand applications that year and the odds of winning were not very good. The Northeast zone is the only one open now, and usually about 200 licenses are allowed.

We bought the license as soon as we were notified that our application had been drawn, and attended a mandatory orientation put on by the Department of Natural Resources. We chose the Tofte location and had our license validated. A close friend of one of the O'Connor brothers, a seasoned pilot who was instrument rated, highly qualified, and part owner of a Cessna 180, agreed to fly us up for the orientation, and my youngest son Terry left his car at the Devil Track airport above Grand Marais for us to use. As soon as we landed, we took his car to Grand Marais for lunch, and then drove to Tofte to attend the orientation. My hunting buddy, who was a member of the party, was unable to meet us up there and took his orientation in the Twin Cities. The game plan for the following day was for the pilot to fly us over our hunting area to look it over. However, when checking on the weather, the pilot was advised to leave as soon as possible because a heavy fog bank was moving in. Hence, he decided to leave and return to the Twin Cities. About seven miles after take off we entered the fog. At times we could not see the lights on the wing tips. The pilot kept in constant contact with radar installations for a triangle fix as to our exact location and altitude all the way back to Anoka County Airport, a flight of about 320 miles. About ten miles from the airport, we broke out of the fog as fast as we had entered it. Because of fog conditions we were put in a holding pattern for over an hour, allowing other small planes that were low on fuel to land ahead of us. This was quite an experience. Because of our pilot's caution and experience, however, we were never in danger.

CALLING THE BULLS AND THE BIG FIGHT

I purchased a recording of Moose calling during their mating season and took several weeks to train my vocal cords to reach the tone and sound levels of their calls. I became really effective at calling on both hunting trips. During the rut, the bulls' hormones take control of their brains, so if it sounds close to the call of the female, they will respond in positive ways. At times you can hear them at dusk, rapping their horns against the trees. I am told that this tells the cows how large he is, and is a means of warning other bulls to stay clear of this area. Often they will work their way downwind of you to pick up the scent of the cow that is calling. At any rate, it works great to call several times about five minutes apart just at dusk, then to be back at the same place in the early light the next morning, make only one loud call then shut up and wait in total silence. If your calling is good and there is a bull in the area, odds are he will show up looking for that lonely cow.

In 1988, we had chosen the zone north and east of where the Brule River crosses under Highway #61. The weekend before season, I went up to scout the area and became familiar with the roads, trails and logging operations past and present that would be helpful in the future. My nephew, Grant, who lives in

Grand Marais and really knows the whole county very well, agreed to spend the day with me and show me some of the places where many moose are seen, on the clear cuts, rivers and trails. We drove over 100 miles that day, mostly on old rutted skid trails and logging roads. We saw nineteen moose that day, including only one small bull with about a thirty inch spread. However, we witnessed two large cows on a clear cut area about seventy-five yards off the trail. They were settling a dispute like a couple of prize fighters, dancing on their hind legs, and sparring and swatting with their front feet. This went on for a full five minutes. The blows they connected with their hoofs were so loud they could have been heard for at least a mile. The older and somewhat larger cow landed a solid blow to the right ear of the younger cow, nearly severing it from the head. This ended the fight. The younger cow took off running with its ear dangling and the older cow, a bit slower, was in hot pursuit. They went up the hill, over a ridge and disappeared. All this time, I had my camera on the seat beside me but was so awestruck at what we witnessed that I never thought of taking pictures until it was over. This was a big mistake. The old timers tell me they have never heard of cows fighting, so I missed the golden opportunity of a lifetime.

This scouting proved very beneficial in the days to come, thanks to Grant!

A BEAUTIFUL OPPORTUNITY MISSED BY OVER CONFIDENCE

Early on opening morning in 1988, I dropped Don O'Connor off about two miles from camp on a large, clear-cut hillside. I returned to camp and hurried on foot to the logged area near camp. Walking very quietly on the balls of my feet to simulate the sound of another animal, I found myself in the middle between two cows on my right and two bulls on my left. The bulls were both younger than we had agreed on when we met to finalize our hunting plans. They were about the same size, possibly two and a half years old. The cows were mature adults, one a yearling and the other quite old and turning gray. The four formed a square about 150 yards in size with me in the center. During the rut this is a dangerous situation to be in. I moved slowly, cautiously ahead about 200 yards to a large clump of mature birches. This is virtually no cover at all to an angry moose; however there was no other cover available, so it did give me an element of false security. They watched me with keen interest all the way, the hair on the bulls' backs standing straight up from their necks to mid-back. I was very concerned for my safety, being all alone and in between four large animals.

About another 100 yards farther up, another black shadow emerged and moved to the left along the wood line, but stayed on the edge of the clear cut. This took my attention from the dangerous situation I carelessly found myself in. He was parallel to me when he finally raised his head. He had about a sixty inch spread and nearly perfect horns. He was definitely the matriarch of this area, and he had not noticed me. Although I was still fearful of my position, he had not seen me, and his size would keep the younger bulls from moving this way. I decided to go for it. I took the best shot available, a quartering shot behind the left shoulder, with the .264 Winchester Magnum. His front shoulder folded and he dropped to his knees. He soon regained his footing and took two steps toward the woods. I called once and he turned his head to look back. I am sure he did not see me, as I was motionless in the birches. I took careful aim and shot him in the neck. He dropped and lay motionless on his right side. The second shot was enough to scare the other four and they disappeared into the woods. The big bull's massive horns were high in the air. He was laying about eighty-five yards away in plain sight. I was sure he would stay down until he bled internally and died. I was so sure of myself that I never even went over to check him out and be sure he was dead.

I walked back toward camp to a large log pile. There were no other hunters in the area, so I climbed to the top of the pile and blew my police whistle to signal Doug and Rod. They were watching both ends of a large clear cut three fourths of a mile north of my location. They had heard the bullets hit and the sharp crack of my .264 Magnum; so they knew it was me and were already on their way. When we got back to the site, we found that the bull had got back on his feet and was gone. I found a long hair, probably from behind his shoulder, and about fifteen drops of fresh blood. About an hour after I shot, we started seeing timber wolves. When wolves smell blood, they are attracted to the area, hoping for a free meal. Between the four of us, we saw seven wolves. The presence of wolves generally indicates a fresh kill; however they did not help us locate the moose as we hoped. We spread out and each took a designated area to search for any sign of blood, broken branches, or hoof prints. We found nothing to help us locate the moose. I was determined to find him and would search until I was satisfied that he could not be found. We searched for two full days but never found him.

On the drizzly second day, I got hopelessly lost in strange country and in an area of magnetic fields that played games with my new compass. The drizzle continued all day and after crossing large belly-deep swamps I came out eight miles from my car. I was soaked from cap to boots, so was forced to abandon the search. I was now cold, hungry, very tired, and most of all, disappointed. Yet I still had eight miles to walk on wet, sore feet and think about my stupidity of not checking the bull and giving him a final shot to guarantee he was dead.

On the fourth day the two O'Connor brothers shot a big bull. After it was hit, it located Doug, turned, and started to charge. Don heard the bullet hit and came running just in time to assist in putting it down. The brothers were very fortunate to have had heavy magnum rifles, and with both shooting, the moose made less than twenty-five yards when it went down for good. During the rut, the bulls are very aggressive and fear is not a factor. Every fall several bulls are killed when they become angry at the whistle of a locomotive and come in second best when they challenge it to a fight for territorial rights.

NOW I HAVE A SECOND CHANCE TO REDEEM MYSELF

This year, 2002, I am eligible to apply again for a moose license. 1988 was the last year you could be drawn and still be allowed to apply. I had applied every year that permits were available, still hoping to have another chance. The rules have changed now, so you may apply as a party of two to four hunters on a license. I am the vice president and an active member of the small but very progressive Moose Willow Sportsmen's Club in Swatara, Minnesota, a small community in North Central Minnesota. We would like to have a trophy moose head to display in our future club house. With our four officers applying separately every two years as the State of Minnesota makes the permits available, we have four chances instead of the one if we applied together. So we are naturally prepared to act fast and purchase the license as soon as possible should any of us be lucky enough to be drawn.

MEETING MY HUNTING COMPANION

The current president of the sportsmen's club is employed as an installer of security alarm systems. He was doing a complete installation for a lady who was living alone. Her name was Megg. Megg's husband had passed away two years earlier from cancer. Their two children were grown, married, and had moved away.

Her home had been burglarized three times in the past month. The last time, late at night, the burglar came right into her bedroom. She awakened to see a small light flash across the wall and heard him on hands and knees sliding her purse across the floor and out the door. She lay petrified with fear. When she was sure he was gone, she called the police. Although she is positive who the burglar was, however there was not enough evidence to prosecute.

The next day, a full security system was installed. The installer was our sportsmen's club president. He suggested she may be wise to learn how to shoot and purchase a hand gun. Megg was interested so he asked me to give her a call...I called her that same evening. A few days later, I had to go into town so I called again and we met for coffee. This was how I first met Megg. Later, I asked her if she would like to go on a Minnesota moose hunt, a once in a life time adventure. Since she was always bubbling with enthusiasm, and we got along so well, I felt that she would be an exceptional hunting companion.

When I called to tell her I received my notice, she asked. "Did you ever doubt it? I knew we would get it." What a positive force! To show my appreciation, I found a cap and couldn't resist buying it for her. The cap was a moose head of dark brown fuzzy material, with nose, eyes, ears, and most important, horns. Being quite naive to this outdoor lifestyle, she actually partially believed she was to wear this cap to be a decoy, as one of the avid hunters had mentioned as much. Everyone had picked up on it, and for quite some time she actually didn't know whether it is true or not. Her brother asked if I had taken out a big insurance policy on her for the trip. He said she was really brave to be taking on such a dangerous assignment. We really had her going and she was a great sport about the whole ordeal. Megg's family gave her three days before she would be begging one of them to come and get her out of the woods and the cold. Two weeks later she actually cried on the way back. She had thoroughly enjoyed the trip, but had to go back to work, while I had to return to finish processing the meat.

PREPARING FOR SUCCESS

My first action was to call Ken Asproth, a top-line taxidermist known world wide for his detail to perfection and in capturing expressions. He took many national awards, and in world competition took several first place awards, including the coveted "Best of Show." Hence, I phoned to make arrangements to have the head mounted. He did not have the facilities to handle ultra-big game, but he gave me three names of quality taxidermists. I chose Taxidermy Unlimited in Burnsville, Minnesota. They do all species of big game from all over the world. Their finished product is so real it looks alive and is actually a work of art.

After a few calls, I reached Marv Gaston, the owner. He reserved a spot for me, although I think he had some doubts. Marv was a bit surprised, to say the least that we are so positive about getting a large trophy, but I guess he liked our confidence and positive attitude. Marv gave me a few pointers on what he would like to have done on the skinning. He then wished us luck and gave me the phone numbers where he could be reached twenty-four hours a day, seven days a week.

Next on the agenda is to purchase a medium size chest freezer, which is secured on my small utility trailer to take with us, to use while processing the meat. Then I dug through my hunting memorabilia to locate the tape on moose calling. I hope my voice has not changed so I can still reach the strong octaves to sound like a moose. Luck is again with me, and in about two weeks I can duplicate the sounds again. Even though I live on forty acres of woods in a remote area and my neighbors are a quarter of a mile away, I practice calling during the day when everyone is at work.

I purchased this forty acre parcel in 1976 because of its game crossings and wild life traffic. It has been a hunting haven for a select few of my friends and family. Everyone looks forward to these few days at an old time deer camp every year. We usually fill out our deer tags.

It was during the time of preparation for our 2001 deer season that I got the call to contact Megg to teach her to become familiar with firearms. She felt safe with her new alarm system connected directly to the police station, so to wait until after deer season is not a problem.

A few days after the close of deer season, I call Megg and we got started. Megg knew nothing about firearms, which is great; she doesn't have any bad habits formed. She is an eager learner and soon became comfortable around guns. I start her with a .22 automatic, then a .410 shotgun. Being involved in hand loading was a real plus. I load some light 110 grains with low velocity for my 30-06 Remington, and then move up a step at a time to full loads. Megg became excited about the sport of shooting. She also became a very good shot, so with this accomplishment and her love of the outdoors. Soon she joined the sportsmen's club and signed up for a ladies' trap team. She accompanied me to Reeds Sporting goods in Walker, Minnesota, where she purchased a Beretta 12 gauge auto loader after looking at a variety of fine shotguns. The louder the roar and the harder the kick, the better she likes it. For beginners I use good ear caps and proper padding so one does not become gun shy. Her favorite rifle is the 30-06 Remington pump, but she also enjoys the .264 Winchester magnum and the .300 Weatherby magnum.

We have been together since our first day, and I am indeed fortunate to have such a wonderful person as my partner and hunting companion. I am retired, sixty-nine years of age, and now have a chance to redeem myself from my screw-up fourteen years earlier, not to mention the whole season to spend in the great outdoors with Megg, a classy, gorgeous lady, the love of my life. So here we are with the chance of a lifetime.

OUR ZONE VS THE BOUNDRY WATERS CANOE AREA

The timing is perfect to be in the north woods during the brilliant fall color change so we can enjoy the beauty. Win, loose or draw, we can never apply for a moose license in Minnesota again, as it is now a once in a lifetime drawing. We chose Zone Seventy where only five licenses are given in the area, from the Brule River east to the Canadian border and north of the Grand Portage Reservation. I know this area well and have seen many moose through the years, some with large trophy antlers. We are very confident in getting a trophy. Some areas have many licenses available, however mostly in the Boundary Waters Canoe Area. Most hunters will apply in the zones with the most available licenses, some up to twenty-five. These are generally in the deeper regions of the BWCA where there are no roads or trails, and can only be reached by canoe and portaging.

These areas are definitely not for sissies. For safety reasons, the D.N.R. (Department of Natural Resources), recommends a party of four for these remote areas. If you can visualize loading all the gear you will need for a two week stay for four people in the cool to cold north wilderness in the fall of the year. Loading the canoes, two, three or four, however many it takes for all the gear and the hunters for a twenty to forty mile journey across lakes, ponds, and rivers, two, three, or more portages, often up to a dozen and some over a mile... you get the picture. Now add the guns, ammunition, canoe paddles, tents, tarps, ropes, block and tackle, rolls of poly, hand axe, knives, sharpening stones, large baggies, pepper and cheesecloth to keep the flies away, coolers for food for four for two weeks, plus the food. You'll need ammonia to ward off bears, a large first aid kit with lots of band aids, and cigarette lighters. Guides are prohibited, so don't forget the maps & compasses, lanterns and flashlights, batteries and gasoline in plastic. Remember, you will all need a minimum of three complete changes of clothing with ponchos, parkas and rain gear. Lots of food, spices, oil, pots and pans, large and small flatware, plates and cups, thermoses for coffee and at least four to six large coolers for bringing the meat out. And don't forget the cameras and film. Remember you will make several trips and probably have at least a dozen portages, some one mile or longer, in a race against time to prevent the meat from spoiling. All gear and garbage that is not burnable must be taken out with you. Glass and metal containers are not allowed at all. You have no choice once you start but to go all the way. You must get this huge animal gutted, skinned, cut up and cooled immediately or it will start spoiling within twenty-four hours, depending on weather conditions, which at this time of the year generally means cold and wet.

If you shoot a moose just at sundown on a lakeshore or riverbank, which is a common situation and is your worst nightmare of bad luck, it will be very dark in a few minutes. The moose will usually end up in about three feet of water. You can't move 1400 pounds by hand, and power equipment of any kind is prohibited and not allowed in the Boundary Waters Canoe Area for any reason.

Two-way radios are also illegal. The moose will have to be cut in pieces small enough to handle, in total darkness, while nearly belly deep in three-plus feet of ice water. Some times the weather will be below freezing and you'll be soaked by chilling sleet and rain. Does this sound like fun? Maybe, but more generally once in a lifetime is sufficient. I know many people who were a part of a team who chose that route. I know only one brave enough to try it a second time. This will help you see why we occasionally make reference during our hunt to saying a prayer. for those eager energetic hunters, in the Boundary Waters Canoe Areas, for they surely do need all the help they can get.

THE SCENIC TRIP

My mind came back to reality as we see the four lane expressway from Duluth narrow into two lanes as we enter the quaint old town. Many years ago the businesses were in the front of the homes as Ma & Pa businesses, with Pa working on the railroad, ore boats, or fishing docks while Ma took care of the children and tended the store. When Pa returned home, he would lend a helping hand. Family ties were very strong and neighbors were more like family members helping out. This still reflects the way life is among the old  timers of this awe-inspiring community. On the outer city limits, a few large chain organizations have set up shop with gas stations, a grocery store, quick serve food and lodging. We make a quick pit stop, which by now is necessary, and purchase a large order of chicken with all the extras for lunch and the remainder for tomorrow's lunch. Naturally, my beautiful dog Cinnamon, an Australian Shepard and Collie cross, needs to stretch her legs, do her thing and sniff every shrub, post, and rock in the area. I named her Cinnamon because of her color. She also has the speckled feet of the Australian Shepherd breed, white sox up to her knees with gray speckles.

A short distance farther and we are at Silver Creek Cliff, where a magnificent tunnel over a quarter mile long has been carved directly through the mountain and is beautifully landscaped on both ends. As we emerge the fall colors are noticeable everywhere and will be turning daily until they reach full color in seven to ten days. A few more miles

and we pass through a second tunnel of equal beauty. Lake Superior plays peek-a-boo through the trees as we continue up the shoreline.

We turn into Gooseberry Park and purchase a detailed map of the entire area in which we will be hunting. This map shows every logging skid trail and hiking trail up to date within the past year. This only takes about twenty minutes and we are back on the highway again.

We cross Gooseberry River Bridge, with its observation decks overlooking the scenic falls below. We have driven down to the park on previous trips to observe this display of natural elegance. It is absolutely gorgeous, as are many of the falls on the North Shore. Soon we pass the driveway to the Split Rock Lighthouse. This served to warn the ocean vessels of the dangerous reefs and rocks in the early days. It was used for both shipping and fish-

ing vessels, as well as the passenger ship (the America) which was the only means of reaching the villages along the way, with stopping points at Grand Marais, Grand Portage, Isle Royal and Canada from this direction. Many ships have met their doom and were sent to the bottom in this vicinity. A book listing some of the history of the Split Rock Light House is available. Its title is *The Split Rock Lighthouse*. Another book also tells of the many ship wrecks in the stormy waters off Lake Superior's South Shore, titled *Dangerous Coast*. Still several books *Shipwrecks of Lake Superior* and *Lake Superior Shipwrecks* document the many ships that have went to the bottom of the North Shore, on this violent and treacherous lake. It is believed that there are approximately 1000 ships lying on the bottom of Lake Superior. To this day, about ½ of them have never been found. Some are occasionally found accidentally by divers and fishermen. This location around the Split Rock Light House is also the location used for some of the filming of two popular movies *Good Son* and *Iron Will*.

Now we are on to Beaver Bay with a quick stop for a big, old-fashioned ice cream cone at the Big Dipper, and to let Cinnamon out of the wagon to sniff every post and shrub. This is a traditional stop. Here at The Big Dipper you get the best and largest ice cream cone of anywhere I have found since I was a small boy.

Just beyond Beaver Bay the Grandpa Woo II is anchored. This is a modern, state-of-the-art tour and excursion boat. The original "Grandpa Woo I" had mechanical trouble with its rudder in 1996 and the stage was set for the treacherous water of Lake Superior to claim another victim. The skipper dropped anchor near Grand Portage. The rudder was removed and sent in for repairs. A bad storm whipped up before it could be replaced, the anchor chain malfunctioned and the Grandpa Woo was adrift The Coast Guard was called, and while fighting strong winds, turbulent seas and extremely dangerous condition, they managed to get a tow line attached. The Coast Guard headed for shelter with the Grandpa Woo in tow. As the storm intensified, the tow line broke. After repeated attempts to reattach a line, it became too dangerous to continue. The remaining crew was lifted to safety and a short time later on October 30th, and some twenty miles downwind, the Grandpa Woo joined the shipwrecks on the rocky shores of Isle Royal, a National Park owned by Michigan. There are at least ten others in this vicinity that have been found. Many divers flock to this area to explore the ancient wrecks. Two of the most noteworthy are the Gunilda, a 200-foot steel luxury yacht, off Rossport, Ontario in 1911. In 300 feet of water, many men have lost their lives trying to salvage the Gunilda. The Chester A. Congdon, a 532-foot freighter, went down in November 1918, off Isle Royale.

Within the entry to Washington Harbor on Isle Royal, and visible on clear days, lies the America, the early means of transportation between Two Harbors and Canada up until it struck a reef in 1928 and sank. The America was the ship that delivered all of the materials for the Split Rock Light House construction and was the only means of transportation for the early settlers farther north.

Back on Highway# 61, The North Shore Drive, we see, from a bluff overlooking Lake Superior, a new modern marina between Beaver Bay and Silver Bay. A large variety of boats, yachts, cruisers and sail boats owned by private parties are docked here, along with an assortment of fishing boats and cabin cruisers. These are used for lake trout and salmon fishing during the summer fishing boom. Just past the marina is the huge taconite facility built in the early and mid-1950's by Reserve Mining at Silver Bay, which was later closed down when it was discovered that asbestos tailings with dangerous levels of cancer-causing fibers were contaminating the water. From here the world's major amount of iron ore called taconite is processed and shipped to steel mills all over the world. This port and loading docks were the frequent loading point for the now famous Edmund Fitzgerald. During an early November storm, with a full load of taconite, the large 729-foot Fitzgerald could not withstand the terrible stress as the weather intensified. They headed for shelter in White Fish Bay, and just a few miles from safety on November 9, 1975, bridging across tremendous waves and swells, the Fitzgerald broke in two and sank, taking all twenty-nine crewmen to their watery grave. This tragedy was recorded by Gordon Lightfoot in the song "The Wreck of the Edmund Fitzgerald."

A short distance farther we passed the docks of Erie mining at Taconite Harbor. The breakwater placed here was formed by huge rock chunks that were blasted off Carlton Peak, which was the highest point in Minnesota and hauled down by flat-bed semis one at a time and placed to form this huge harbor. During the process of loading and moving these giant, jagged pieces of rock that weighed about twenty ton each, many flat beds were flattened and crushed. The giant tongs on the crane would slip because of the extreme weight. The crumbly texture of the rock, and the squared configuration didn't give the tongs much to grip. When the rock dropped, the trailer collapsed, causing total destruction. The frames were reinforced and a bed of old tires were placed on the deck but this was still not very effective with the massive weight involved. On the way down the steep incline, many times the chain binders would break or slip, brakes would fail, and icy roads, and bad weather and other variables made it almost impossible to find truck drivers desperate enough to risk their lives for regular driver pay. Also, insurance cancellation and destruction of trucks brought the project to a slowdown and complete halt on more than one occasion. At one point, the general contractor purchased five new trucks, to keep the project going. However, the trucking contractor, already bankrupt because of this project, refused to accept them until the conditions were renegotiated.

The next small town is Shroeder, where a small shop featuring scrimshaw articles (bone and antler ear rings and necklaces) are available for sale. They also have many miscellaneous natural minerals and forest products, from which is created beautiful jewelry.

As we leave Schroeder we enter Tofte, another small town that was once a fishing village when the lake trout harvest was at its peak. A beautiful large resort/motel, the Blue Fin, now sits right on the shore of Lake Superior.

Another point of interest just beyond Tofte is Minnesota's oldest resort, The Lutsen Resort and Ski Hills. This is where Cindy Nelson lived and trained for the many events she starred in. She was the first American to gain world recognition (downhill racing in 1974), and went on to capture the world Olympics bronze in 1978. We will return to the Ski Hills accommodations next weekend for a three day rest and relaxation at Caribou Highlands. Looking up the hillside across the highway we can see the magnificent golf course. It is very picturesque, with the bright green fairways bordered by yellow and orange aspen and dotted with red oaks, clumps of blood red sumac, and patches of evergreens. When we return next weekend it should be in full color.

Five miles from Grand Marais is the large man-made rock-cut and observation area overlooking Lake Superior. From the overlook we can see the Grand Marais Harbor, lighthouse and Coast Guard Station, some small islands and often small boats fishing for trout and salmon. The water here is a bright blue, absolutely fascinating. This area of shoreline is the location of Thompsonite gem stones and there is only one other area in the World that has them, somewhere in Argentina. About a quarter mile farther, on the lake shore, is a new wayside rest with natural stone barricades, bathrooms and picnic tables. This is another place to observe the beauty of natural products wisely incorporated into the fascinating landscape of the North Shore Drive.

Ten minutes later we are entering the city limits of Grand Marais. A few new businesses and motels have sprung up on the outskirts of town, but as a whole it remains as inviting as it was on my first visit here over fifty years ago. As we break over the hill, most  of Main Street is in view, as well as the scenic harbor. This gorgeous view broadens as we get closer to the spectacular enclosed harbor. The Coast Guard Station with the breakwater and light house are a sight to be long remembered. The fisherman's wharf and the small restaurant, The Angry Trout, looks as if it were 100 years old and it may well be original.

Lake Superior has a very nasty disposition when the late fall waves churn up the icy waters into huge, crushing waves. During one of these storms, I witnessed huge rocks and boulders being thrown over the curbs onto the public parking lot in front of the Coast Guard Station. This storm destroyed the lake side of a home, totally eliminating the large three season porch, causing the elderly lady to  flee for her life. Another storm flooded the entire lower areas of Grand Marais with two or more feet of water.

On the upper side of Highway# 61 is the Gunflint Trail and the entry point to the Boundary Waters Canoe Area. Everyone without exception must obtain a permit to have access by water to this pristine wilderness, and only a limited number of permits are issued at a given time.

OUR BASE CAMP

Two miles east of Grand Marais is our base for our big hunt. I have a converted school bus permanently parked on the back of private property beyond the home of Dean and Marietta Berneking. They have allowed me to keep the bus there for over ten years. The Bernekings are the kind of folks whom you meet only once in a lifetime. I have been blessed with the good fortune to have known them for over twenty-five years. They raised twin boys who are an example to everyone who knows them. They have excelled academically, as well as in many sports, and their walls are covered with ribbons, plaques and trophies including three gold medals, for the three years they took back-to-back state high school football championships. All three years were decided in double and triple overtime. The family is well-known and respected throughout Cook County and many other areas of the state.

We unload and get organized while Cinnamon enjoys getting out and running. Megg got everything put away and in its place while I hook up the electric extension cords, turn on the gas, lite the furnace, fill the porta-potti and fill our water containers. In less than an hour we are all set up. We then stop to say hello to a few friends and ask about the moose areas that I am familiar with. We mentally made our plan for tomorrow and chart our course to drive and get familiar with the new clear cuts and logging trails where we will be hunting on opening day. The word is clear from everyone that there are a lot of moose everywhere, especially in the burned area on our western boundary over by Powers Lake. This is useful information for later, but I know the easterly area well and will still try for one of the huge bulls in this area first.

We turn in early to get rested up for a fast start tomorrow. We want to be out early since the moose is a nocturnal animal and are often seen on the roads just before daylight and just after dark. This early in the season, the moose are out feeding and browsing, but are not in the rut for another week yet. However, their tracks are visible in the gravel on the sides of the blacktop. This is a good indication of the best areas of population and size of the moose.

Friday, September 27

I get up at 4:00 A.M., put on the coffee and pack our chicken and some snacks. After pouring two cups of coffee, the remainder goes in the thermos and a second pot is perking. The fresh smell of perking coffee in the northern wilderness helps me get a bit of life going as Megg responds to an all new world of excitement and anticipation. It is 4:45 A.M., even Cinnamon knows something different is brewing. I let her out to relieve herself, as she will be left alone in the bus until we return about noon. We fill the thermos and have a warm up. There is still enough for two cups in insulated mugs to enjoy on the way.

We leave about 5:10 A.M., drive East on Highway# 61 for about sixteen miles, then going north we make a double loop of the roads in this area. There are not as many fresh tracks on the gravel roads as we had hoped for, but it is still definitely good in some areas. We return to camp at 11:15 A.M. and let

Cinnamon out for her exercise run, then we load her in the wagon and go to Grand Marais for an excellent breakfast at S.O.B., South of

the Border Restaurant. Upon returning back to the bus, we tie Cinnamon outside while we take a one hour nap. This is necessary if we are to remain alert during the late afternoon hours.

24

Friday P.M.

At 2:15 P.M. we head out again. About four miles east of camp we saw a DNR (Department of Natural Resources) pickup stopped on the shoulder of Hwy# 61 facing us. The driver was using a cell phone. We stop and I cross the highway to talk to him. It turns out he is the local game warden and is very pleasant to talk to. He gives me a lot of valuable information which proves to be beneficial and advises that the westerly portion of our zone is loaded with big bulls. He says our chances of getting a trophy rack will probably be better there. We go over our map and he points out where he has seen large bulls and the time of day he has seen them. He likes the idea that we are organized and pretty well-informed, and seems very eager to help us bag a large trophy. He suggests that we hunt over by Powers Lake.

Two years ago, in 2000, a severe forest fire had burned hundreds of acres. There was no new growth of brush or timber in this area. The fire had been so hot that it had burned all of the soil off the rocks and left them white from the heat. The rains had washed the rocks clean and left no soot or ashes. The stumps were nearly all burned off at ground level. This had forced all wildlife, including the moose, to move to the surrounding areas near the lakes and water for protection when the fire went through. Because of the lack of vegetation, the wildlife stays clear of this area. However, the moose have a tendency to move out to open areas during the rut. This may be to our advantage in the future. However, I have also seen several very large bulls in the past years off the Otter Lake Road and on the Swamp River flowage. We have hopes of seeing a large bull on one of the many clear-cut areas or in the slashings left by logging. We also have the many logging roads, skid trails and landings to check out.

All guns have been sighted in and are ready. Megg wants to use my Remington Model 760 30-06 with 220 gr. round nose Hornady bullets. I want her to do the shooting, and she feels comfortable with the 1 ½ x 4 Bushnell combination, with the range compensator. I will probably use the 300 Weatherby Magnum with a Leopold 3 x 9. Both of these rifles are exceptionally accurate, and pack a heavy punch with deep penetration. We also have with us a Weatherby .264 Winchester Magnum and a Browning automatic .300 Winchester Magnum, both with quality scopes.

Opening Day

Saturday, September 28

I am up at 4:00 A.M. and hit the button on the coffee pot. I let Cinnamon out to run and sniff while I place the guns and supplies in the station wagon, as neatly and organized as permissible. The coffee is poured and the lunch is loaded. I awaken Megg at 4:45 A.M. With her clothes all laid out, she is ready in ten minutes. We will drink our coffee on the way. Grouse season & duck season also open today. My buddy Rod and his good friend Brian are out in the lot and getting ready to go up to Swamp River hunting ducks. We stop for a few minutes to give them our game plan. They believe we will get our moose this first weekend, and they want to be available to help us with the extremely hard job of handling over 1400 pounds of dead weight in field dressing and to help get it out. We hope they are right. After finding out what their plans are and where they will be if we should need their help. We head out. The excitement is at a high level.

As we turn onto Highway# 61, Megg asks me if this is dangerous. Her family has heard many stories of how dangerous moose, as well as other wildlife, can be in northern Minnesota. The big concern is the aggressiveness of the bull moose during mating season. I have assured them I will not leave her alone, and now I reassure her that we will be within sight of each other all the time.

But I did tell her how dangerous moose can be if one were to let their guard down and get careless or foolish. Her family is aware that I have had considerable experience with wild animals in a lifetime of hunting. I have to agree, wild animals are very dangerous and have incredible power. Moose, deer, bear and timber wolves are all unpredictable even if not wounded, but if they feel cornered, whether intentional or not, they are exceedingly dangerous. In 1996, my dog Cinnamon was attacked by a pair of timber wolves. Fortunately, my .41 magnum Ruger Black Hawk saved us from the attack. I fired when the male was about three feet away and sailing thru the air with fangs bared right for my throat. A 911 call was made moments before. There is no way the call would be of any benefit, but my .41 neutralized the situation. But that's another story. It seems that if the unusual is going to happen, it always happens to me or around me. For this reason, I will never let my guard down.

A MISSED OPPORTUNITY FOR A MONSTER TROPHY

We turn north on the Arrowhead Trail. A couple more turns and we arrive at a slashing at about 5:45 A.M. I quietly step out, load our guns, set them beside the wagon for quick action, call three times then wait. I try several more times and nothing shows up or answers.

As the sun came up bright, it is a memorable fall morning. Grouse season has just opened today and a lot of road hunters start driving back and forth looking for grouse. This is not to our advantage. All of this road activity has disrupted our plan and virtually destroy our chances of walking the skid trails. We unload our rifles, case them and start driving to check out some landings farther off the beaten path.

I see my ex-brother-in-law's camper trailer in a gravel pit next to the road and seeing that his pick up is there, we decide to stop and say hello. As we leave, we decide to drive to other areas, so we will leave a note on Rod's windshield, at the Swamp River landing. He and his hunting buddy, Brian Peterman, are duck hunting and will need to know where we are should they decide to come looking for us. With our change in plans we make more room in front and place the guns and shells in the back of the wagon. This turns out to be a big mistake. We didn't expect to see a trophy bull at this time of the day this early in the season.

We had only gone about a mile when, rounding a bend, there was a small clearing on a huge flat rock with a large, wide evergreen on the far right side. The evergreen is exceptionally dark so we didn't notice the moose until he walked out from behind it. "There's our trophy!" I said excitedly, "Oh no! One of his horns is missing. But, wow, look at the size of him, and look at the size of that panel." The rear panel is about four feet long and eighteen inches wide with many points, and about five to six points at least six inches long on the forward panel. The forward points are polished and actually glisten as he moves cautiously forward. The main panel is a beautiful dark chestnut high above his graying ears and head.

We stop in an area of dark brush cover so the wagon is only partly exposed above the brush line. I'm sure he doesn't see us. As we watch we make no effort to get the guns. He is not our trophy with only one horn. Then he steps totally out and turns his head away from us, and there in front of us is a huge monster bull...the trophy we have dreamed about, and he has both horns. I did not remember that a moose will not break a horn off, the skull will break before the horn, killing the animal. His hide is a shiny jet black with some graying over his shoulders and around his ears. As he walks out, he has turned his head; we can't help but notice he has a large beard nearly a foot long. I know he will weigh at least 1,600 pounds and have at least a five-and-half foot spread.

I whisper, "Stay behind the door, move beyond the second door and be as quiet as you can before opening it, and stay down behind the door. I'll hand you your gun."

I move quickly on my side and hand Megg her gun but can't locate the clips. I will have to open the back lid to get the clips out of her parka. Now the moose sees us and stops momentarily, then walks out past the brush line. Time is running out. He continues walking as he watches us. I see a box of 300 Weatherby shells on the back seat and grab two out of the box, as I pull the Weatherby forward to the back seat and out of the case. The bolt is closed so this takes extra time to get it open and stuff in the two shells. I step out from behind the doors, across the road and into the woods. The moose also walks into the woods and turns away from me. Why didn't he turn towards me I wonder, which being curious in nature, is what I expect him to do, but wildlife nearly always does the unexpected. As I threw the gun to my shoulder, his graying hump and rump disappear. He is about 100 yards away and in an open enough area that I could have got a fairly decent shot at him if he only turns toward us. I run down that way but he is gone...a golden opportunity missed by my stupidity.

The inside pad on his worn hoof measures 5 3/8 inches, as compared to that of the big trophy we later bagged, which measures 3 5/8 inches. By not practicing a dry run of what to do and how to proceed in a sudden situation, we had just missed a chance of 100 lifetimes. This was a huge bull with massive antlers, the second largest bull I have ever seen. I had really goofed and caused us to loose out...totally my fault, for which I have no excuse.

When we reach the Swamp River landing, I decide that this is a good place to correct the error. We proceed to practice fast moves to uncase the rifles efficiently and have everything in place to be quickly accessible. When we are both comfortable with this procedure, we again case the guns and place them for quick action. We then leave a note for the boys on their windshield telling them where we are going.

We check out several other logging roads and sled trails and become familiar with the surroundings. We have walked at least five miles by the time we return to the station wagon. We drive north on the Swamp River Road and Otter Lake Road, carefully looking for moose and other signs. We again intercept the McFarland Lake road and continue to the Shoe Lake Road and follow it across the north end of our zone to the sign marking the zone boundaries. There are moose tracks all over the road, which is immensely encouraging.

We continue on and turn into view the Greenwood Lake helicopter pad. This is absolutely awesome country and the view is breath taking from this high vantage point. In the near future we will return to Greenwood Lake to fish for walleye, lake trout and northern pike. Many record class fish in all three species have been caught in Greenwood for many years.

We continue west to the Gunflint Trail, then back down to camp, where we let Cinnamon out to stretch, sniff and squat. She sure is happy to see us. We make a quick sandwich and enjoy a few minutes of relaxing with a coke, then it is time to be on the road again and check out another long skid trail and hunt till dark. There are not a lot of fresh signs on the landing, but the northerly skid trail has a super good crossing along a creek bed. We stay there until 6:30 P.M. I call a few times with no response and we leave for camp.

We do a quick change of clothes and head to Grand Marais for the American Legion's special half chicken dinner, which is very tasty. We can not help but share our deep appreciation for the warm surroundings and the convenience of a good meal without all the work. Those poor guys in the Boundary Waters Canoe Area have to settle for beans and hamburgers or hot dogs over an open fire. I would bet they are having a great time for the first couple of days. It won't be quite as much fun in the morning getting the fire going and fixing coffee and breakfast in the dark, damp and cold air. And it will get to be more work as the days go by.

We swap a few tales with some of the old timers and absorb another earful of advice from past experiences. One can sure learn a lot by listening to those who have a lifetime of backwoods knowledge. At about 10:00 P.M., we return to the bus and fix coffee and sandwiches for tomorrow. We arrange our clothing and necessaries for a quick start in the morning and retire. We are still chuckling about the B.S. that was passed around at the Legion while we were eating.

During the evening one of my old friends from years back had said that we were the only ones guaranteed a trophy bull… just put out the word and he could have a hundred "good" hunters out there within a couple of hours to shoot a "real trophy" for us.

I replied, "I doubt if you even know one 'good hunter', but by your standards, I suppose anyone would seem good." I would like to mention your name but after you read this, you will know who I mean. Everyone got a laugh out of that. Naturally, I decline the offer for their help. This is our mission, and we are confident that we will succeed. Incidentally, the guy who made this offer is one of the best woodsmen I have every known, however, I would never tell him this to his face, as it would spoil his image of me.

Day 2

Sunday, September 29

Rod had previously said he would let Cinnamon out at noon, so we would not have to return and could stay out all day. Rod's long time friend and hunting companion, Brian, offered us the use of his 4 x 4 Ford pickup. We could drive in and check out the logging roads that are two-plus miles long and not have to walk both ways. We can cover twice the area this way and not be quite as tired. We have covered many miles in the morning and didn't find any new promising areas.

About noon, we decide to head west over by Powers, Esther and Chester Lakes on the other side of our zone. This is the area where we bagged our bull in 1988, fourteen years ago, and where hundreds of acres of prime moose country had burned two years earlier. This has forced all wildlife to run for their lives. The moose congregated in dense wooded areas around the burn out. With the cover burned, many of the roads have now washed out and many of the skid trails are impassible or could not be recognized. The whole area is drastically altered. What had been swamps are now dry.

Nothing is familiar in this baron desolate area, and I have very little idea as to where we really are. At one point, we back up a mile as the road became absolutely impossible to drive on. In this area of magnetic fields, a compass becomes radical, is not dependable, and can not be trusted. This is the area that had me confused and very lost because of the magnetic fields back in 1988.

With this issue still lingering in my mind, I am again uncertain as to the several options in roads, better described as trails, that we should take. The clouds have the sun totally hidden and we are absolutely lost once again. We follow one narrow road or trail about a mile, only to find another older gentleman stopped at a big washout. The evergreens are so dense and the road so narrow that one can not see to back up. He wants to go back. We help get him turned around and heading back. I tell him where we are camped, and he agrees to check and see if we make it back. If we don't, he will send someone after us. He seems to know where we are.

I can't go back because we are too low on fuel to make it. We carried the rocks from below the washout and replace them carefully so we can get through. In low range and four wheel drive, we inch slowly up the long grade. The rocks held in place all the way up. Once on top, though now what? We could see the land sloped down, so this has to be toward Lake Superior. With the other gentleman gone, we both felt as if we were in this vast area abandoned and alone.

Farther ahead we came upon a swamp with flowing water across the road. Megg walked ahead of the truck for about a fourth of a mile picking the trail, with me inching behind her. Another half mile and I recognized a spot I remembered from 1988. This was locally know as Boom Sticks Pond, and is less than a mile from where we bagged our moose back in 1988. Salvation at last!

This has been a real challenging trip. Megg was a true companion today, she never doubted my judgment and gave me consolation and encouragement at every decision. She is worried, as I am, also, but she never complained. It is getting dark and this big swamp looks like a small lake, yet she walks across it a half step at a time, feeling the recesses of the tracks or ruts, to guide us, sometimes nearly a foot deep. I doubt if most men would have been so brave. Beyond the tracks on both sides is deep muck, in some places possibly four feet deep or more. Megg said this is a rough but fun day, even though we saw no moose. Cinnamon is absolutely wild to see us. The tail is wagging the dog, for sure. Needless to say, we are also very happy to be together again.

I can't help but think about the hunters in the Boundary Waters Cano Area when they become disoriented in the dark on their way back to camp. Many of these hunters are not experienced woodsmen and are accepting their first real challenge in the remote wilderness. One mistake out here can mean big trouble, and has resulted many times in organized search parties. Just as we were ready to turn in for the night, the gentleman we met earlier in the day stopped by to see if we made it. What a nice person. I regret that I do not remember his name.

Day 3

Monday, September 30

We decide to go back to the same areas we started in for at least another three days. About five miles into our hunting zone we round a bend and about thirty yards off to our right is a young cow and a two or three year old bull with a nice even pair of antlers. The width may possibly reach thirty inches but no more. They are both in very good condition and shiny black. They look at us for a brief minute, then before I could get completely stopped, they start walking away along the side hill and climbing higher as they went. I drive ahead slowly to a spot where we can get a better view and stop. We watch their reaction as I call three times with the cow's urgent "come and get me", mating call. They stop and look back. The bull turns and looks as if he wants to come back but the cow moves in front of him. They definitely show a keen interest, but changed their minds and continue along the side hill, up and out of sight.

We could have easily gotten off the logging road, got our guns ready and shot either of them, but we are after a record trophy, and these are not what we are willing to settle for. Maybe on the last day of season our attitude will be different if we still have our license to fill. No question these would be a good choice for our Thanksgiving feast.

This is a good area it has been recently logged, and had an abundant growth of tender saplings. We can see the tops of many are nipped off from moose browsing. This may be a good place to spend a few hours. We pull up about three blocks to a landing, get somewhat out of sight with the wagon, and quietly make ready for a few hours of sitting. Each of us select a large pile of slashings and tops about twenty yards off the trail about fifty feet apart. We climb up on top and position ourselves so we can see each other, see both directions on the trail and still watch the hillside. When we both get comfortably situated, I call twice, wait about fifteen minutes and call again.

I was about to call the third time when I saw Megg come to attention looking up the hillside. A two year old bull with a pair of antlers like turkey platters about eighteen to twenty-four inches apart was coming along the hillside toward us. He was close to 100 yards away and definitely looking. Megg very quietly motioned and said "Call him again."

I replied, "Are you nuts? He's too close, and he has spotted us."

The hair on his neck and back start standing up and as he proceeds toward us he lays his ears back. He is now about fifty yards away and stops to look us over. I whisper to Megg to get her gun ready but not to shoot. I start shooting pictures as he came closer. The camera would click and wind automatically to the next picture.

He is becoming increasingly upset with every picture. I am lying on my back and taking pictures over my head. At this position I have a hard time following him and keeping him in the lens. With my fourth picture he lays his ears back flat; by now he is only thirty-five yards away. I stop, and let go of the camera, swapping it for the 300 Weatherby.

Seeing this Megg raises her gun, the 30-06 pump, and says, "I'm going to shoot him."

I warn her that this is too close. "Don't you dare, this is dangerous. And he is just a "Bambi."

"I don't care. He's huge, and I'm going to shoot."

Again, very firmly I said, "Don't you dare. It's a Bambi; don't waste our license this early in the season."

He watches our every move and really studies the situation for about ten minutes, which seems like an hour, then walks up the hillside and out of sight…big sigh of relief for me. Much to Megg's frustration and disappointment, this subsequently became nicknamed "Bambi Land."

We stay for about another hour, and then I left Megg near the car just in case one with big horns should come along and cross the landing. I give her firm orders that this was a once in a lifetime opportunity, and under no conditions was she to shoot a Bambi, nothing under forty-eight inches. I then went to the top of the hill. This is very steep and with many logs and tops crossways, almost impossible to climb.

Cutting north along the ridge was no better. The top was worse than the hillside. Out of sight from the road, the loggers had left a terrible mess. I could only go about fifty feet at a time, and then there was another huge brush pile of tops to fight my way through. I stayed parallel with the road for a quarter mile, then head in farther, as it looks better.

This, too, is a real jungle with tree tops in every direction, making it almost impossible to crawl through. Even the skid trails are intentionally piled with tops and brush to prevent passage. After a mile of this, enough is enough. How the moose can get through this mess is beyond me. I fight my way back to the road. This little trip takes over two and a half hours.

Since the colors are changing daily, we drive to the three helicopter pads. These pads give us a beautiful view of the tree tops from above, two of them overlooking the Pigeon River and both sides of the Canadian border, and the third overlooking

Greenwood Lake. The view from the southerly helicopter pad overlooking the Pigeon is breathtaking. You can see the Pigeon for miles as it winds through the swamps and valleys towards Lake Superior. The hillsides on both sides are glowing with color. The helipads are helicopter landing pads built by the government on high points for emergency use to bring in fire fighters and supplies and transport campers and civilians out, with the hope they will never be used. This is an area of devastating blow-down some fifteen miles wide and sixty miles long… a tinder box for forest fires. The imminent danger is not if, but when the fire will happen, and how many will perish that can't get out and how many will die fighting the fire. This can very likely be the site of the greatest fire the state, and possibly the nation will ever have. From these pads the scenery is absolutely gorgeous all summer long, but is unequalled for beauty when it is in full color. This became a daily stop off, as each day is more spectacular than the day before. Words cannot describe the real true splendor, so few people have ever witnessed from this vantage point.

We take many pictures of this unparalleled panoramic view. It will take at least thirty years or longer for regrowth to take place and return this gorgeous country to the natural pristine wilderness it once was. Megg and I realize we may never again have the opportunity to view the true beauty as it reaches its mature color; one day at a time and all day long, so we decide we must return and witness this phenomenal transformation day by day. We are truly blessed with this opportunity to spend the entire fall season, in the season of our lives, in a once-in-a-lifetime moose hunt, to see everything unfold with a new and different thrill and experience every day. We can hunt all day today and do not have to return at noon, since Brian offered to let Cinnamon out and take her for a walk. We drive about ten miles to the end of the Otter Lake road then back to the Jackson Lake Road, turning off to Lake Andy. At the end of the road we park and walk back in about two miles, looking for tracks and other signs. There are several small landings and many older tracks, but nothing really fresh. On the way out, the other side of the road looks a lot better. We stop and talk to several local hunters who are driving the roads looking for ruffed grouse. All of them report seeing moose in this area in the past three days. We drive slowly looking for tracks on the way back to Highway# 61, and return to camp early.

Dean Berneking has finished up a job and came home a little earlier than usual, so we have a chance to chat for a little while. Dean's property is where the bus is parked. Dean works all over the area and covers a lot of ground, doing road building, excavations and sewer work. He also is an avid sportsman. He confirms that there are moose everywhere but that he has not seen any big bulls recently, although his drivers occasionally report seeing one and where it was at. He tells me there isn't a need to walk on the balls of my feet, as it is not possible to stalk up on a moose because of their big ears, good hearing and other keen senses. I take great pride in my stalking ability since I have stalked up to within a few feet of deer on several occasions and up to fifty feet of a timber wolf when I was younger. I will challenge this, the first chance I get.

Day 4

Tuesday, October 1

The forecast is for another warm, clear, fall day. We leave camp at 5:00 A.M. to get out in the woods and on stand while it is still dark. Because of the clear weather, it is getting light a few minutes earlier than normal. We proceed to the open hillsides on the Lake Andy Road and park the wagon off the road and take stands behind some big cedars so we can cover the feeding spots on the hillside.

Daylight came, what a beautiful day, but no moose show up. There are moose tracks all over the road, all of them fresh. All of the grouse road hunters, without exception, have seen moose here, but not us. On several occasions the moose tracks are over the car tracks that we made on our way in. The road is only three miles long. The trip in and out only takes ten minutes.

We drive back to the Otter Lake Road, past Bambi Land, and turn right on a landing road about one mile before Otter Lake. About half a mile in is a large clear landing that has just been logged closer to the road. However, it has been logged farther in over several hundred acres within the past two or three years. This is ideal moose browse. There is still a log pile of large birch, which is about ten feet high and contains about forty cords of saw logs.

On the landing are several short trails and two abandoned logging trails, one to the left and one past the log pile to the right. We walk the one to the left for about two miles. The ruts are so deep it is even difficult to walk.

A 4 x 4 ATV will not be able to travel this route. About a half mile from the landing, the road dips down and crosses a wet mucky river bed about twenty feet wide. We have to walk back in the woods to cross the water. There are a lot of fresh moose tracks in the muck and on both sides of the water flowage. All of these are large tracks...this is truly big bull country.

A half mile beyond the wet spot are a couple hundred acres that had been logged two to three years earlier. Bear hunters have a high stand and two feeding or baiting stations about fifty yards on either side of the trail. I climb the stand to have a look. It is so grown up that it is at least a year past its usefulness. Although you may be able to spot a moose from here, it is doubtful you would be able to get a bullet thru the new growth of aspen. This may be a good spot in a few years after a lot of the weaker trees have smothered and died out, however, the logging road has already became a game trail. There are about a dozen very large dead trees where one could place a stand and be able to cover some of the smaller game trails that cross the ridge. Hopefully, a moose might walk out on the main game trail.

This will be a good vantage point to call from. It would also be a bad place to pack out your game, but we joke about this being a lot easier than the portages faced by the hunters in the Boundary Waters Canoe Area.

We return to the low area and watch the trail for two hours before returning to camp. On the way, we stop at the southerly heliport to view the beautiful colors and recharge our enthusiasm.

Back at camp, Cinnamon is anxious to get out in the fresh fall air and enjoy her exercise. We doze outside in the lawn chairs for about an hour, with Cinnamon happy to just be beside us.

About 1:00 P.M. we leave camp. Since it is such a beautiful day we decide to go back to the Lake Andy road to the trails at the end. We walk the logging road to the west for a couple of miles to a higher ridge. This was logged a few years earlier. There are cedar swamps just beyond the ridge. Many large crooked cedars have been left standing because they are too twisted and crooked to be sawn for lumber, and many large logs have been left scattered along the sides of the clearing. They are hollow or gnarly, so can not be used. This is ideal moose habitat. Moose tracks and droppings are everywhere. We are astonished to see the size and number of moose beds, on this grassy open ridge. In an area about forty yards wide and 200 yards long we count forty-nine beds, all made this fall.

We take stands a few yards apart so we can each see for 150 yards, plus both ways on the main trail and seventy-five to one hundred yards down side trails. I call about every half hour but got no response. We wait until the sun drops behind the tallest trees, then start the long walk back through rough ground and swampy areas. At times the brush and alders have grown together, so one can see only a few yards ahead. This is not a real good situation to be in during the moose rutting season. In these close quarters, one can be within twenty feet of a big bull before seeing it…way too close to be safe. A bull during the rut will attack nearly every time, if provoked.

Finally, within a quarter of a mile from the road the trail opens up. Bear hunters have placed a stand and two baiting stations on the two side trails. These they have traveled to with a 4 x 4 ATV. We both breathe a sigh of relief to be out in the open before darkness settles in. I will avoid these closed-in areas if possible, especially during hours of subdued light. I believe this logging trail extends all the way to Swamp River some four miles up stream from the Swamp River Landing. We will definitely come back to check this out, but need an earlier start to be in and back out in full daylight.

Through the years I have seen a dozen or more huge bulls cross the river. In 1969, while duck hunting on Swamp River, my hunting companion and I saw a big bull with a fifty-five inch spread. He was as mad as if he had a hornet under his tail, throwing muck and tundra twenty feet in the air and bellowing steady. He was giving ground and not liking it. His hump and head were all that showed above the swamp brush, and he was a very large bull. We were expecting that a pack of wolves had him on the run, but instead it was a monster bull whose total body was visible above the brush. He must have weighed close to a ton. I estimated his antler spread to be seven to seven and a half feet, and each upper panel to be over fifty inches long. His forward panels had five long points on one side and six on the other. With 10 x 50 binoculars and only about forty yards between us, it was fairly easy to count the points when he stopped and looked at us. He had twenty-two points on each side of his main panels. His antlers laid out flat and they were fairly even. If mounted, he would have been a magnificent trophy. Several other grouse and duck hunters had seen him and they said he had over an eight foot spread. I was a carpenter by trade, and am very familiar with measurements. If this was the same bull they had seen, I doubt if he would have made the eight foot mark. Never the less, he is magnificent.

The next day, Rod and I went up a side flowage with my light twin weed-less outboard motor, propelling us in this little river. It's a good combination. About a strong half mile, we went over three beaver dams. The woods of the channel narrowed to a little more than the width of the canoe. With the twisting and turning it is very difficult to navigate. Upon rounding a bend as I push the canoe forward, Rod stiffened and motioned me to back up. I couldn't for a minute or more, the little three horse weed-less prevented me from backing up, until I removed it and laid it on the brushy bank and I picked up a long paddle. As I pushed the canoe back, Rod looked toward me and whispered there is a big bull, about a canoe length ahead. I could see his outline through the brush, as he shook his horns at us. He charged a few feet, then retreated back to where he was. We quickly and quietly exchanged our shells from fine shot to buck shot. I was fully expecting we would have to kill him in self defense. After three charges, he gave it up and walked away. This is closer to danger than I ever want to be.

Two years earlier, a logger with a small John Deere crawler, in deep snow got hung up on a big bull with massive Antlers, possibly a winter kill. I never had a chance to talk to him personally about this. There is a strain of very large moose in this area. That is a factor in picking this zone. We will come back here again. I am very excited about this being a spot I have wanted to explore for many years. I am sure, if this is the spot I am hoping for, that we will have an excellent chance of bagging an exceptionally large bull just at dusk, by boat or canoe on the river and then can tow it down river to the landing. This will be a hard way to go, but I feel it will just about guarantee a huge trophy.

Day 5

Wednesday, October 2

The weather forecast is for two more days of sunshine, and the colors are turning brighter and more brilliant daily. We return to the area where we were yesterday and continue to the end of the trail. This is the spot that I hoped it would be, well worth the three mile walk. The view from here is beyond words, with Swamp River twisting and winding through the muskeg in areas of bright blue to dark green. Because of the large area of stagnant water, floating bog, and decaying foliage, there is always a haze over the water.

The hills in the background are exploding in color. I brought the camera to capture this scenic feast.

We return to the wagon. With the beauty all around us, we decide to take in as much as we can and still be moose hunting. As we join the Otter Lake Road, Megg is looking left as I turn right towards the heliport to see a very large black timber wolf coming out on the right and run down the road a few yards before crossing the road and running into the woods on the left. I am taking a bite of my sandwich so before I can say anything he is gone. Unfortunately, Megg did not get to see it. Black timber wolves are extremely rare, it would have been a real treat for her to see.

We take some more pictures from the heliport, then discuss our next move and head north again past Otter Lake, turn right on the Arrowhead Road, turn left on the Shoe Lake Road, and two miles up the Shoe Lake Road where we encounter moose tracks like we have never seen before. Although we have not seen the numbers of moose we expected, this is tremendously encouraging. This is still in our zone almost all the way to Greenwood Lake, and this area is famous for big moose. It's just a matter of time until Grandpa Bull-Winkle makes his appearance on our terms. The rut is just starting and the activity is picking up. We are still in no hurry to end this lifetime opportunity and we are very optimistic of shooting a trophy bull. This is beyond doubt the most memorable, breathtaking and fascinating experience that one can ever dream of. Today is for enjoyment and we are soaking in the artistry as we stop atop the Greenwood Lake Lookout. The view from here is absolutely beautiful, with the varied colors blending into picturesque patches down the incline and disappearing behind the curtain of color that conceals the closest shores of the lake somewhere over a mile away. A couple of scenic islands further out complete this perfect landscape. The shores twist and turn in the far distance, and disappear beyond the hills. A few more pictures and we are again on the move to the Gunflint Trail.

We continue down the Gunflint Trail and turn off on the Elbow Lake Road. Just one and a half miles and we are at the picnic area and the public access. As we walk down to the boat landing we observe some bright orange on the point to the right. It appears as if two or three guys are trying to pull a moose up closer to shore. As we watch we can hear voices shouting back and forth to "hurry and get those coolers over here" . . . (again) "hurry up we have a lot to do and we need help now" . . . 'it'll get dark before we get done as it is.'

After a few minutes I walk up to the wagon and got the binoculars. We wanted to see what their big problem is. When I got back with the binoculars and look at the shore…what a shock! I hand them to Megg. She, too, is in total disbelief and amazed. What we have been watching are bright orange overhanging limbs flowing in the wind.

Out of our sight from the boat landing are a group of grouse hunters setting up camp at one of the campsites. We went over and talked to them. They are the ones that we overheard talking and shouting and believed they were moose hunters. We are too embarrassed to tell them what we had mistakenly observed. This proves that seeing is not necessarily believing, what you hear is not always what's happening, and how mistaken you can be when you are in a certain frame of mind and totally involved in a different range of activity. To say the least, we felt downright stupid.

When we leave here, we drive back out to the Gunflint Trail and continue down to the Mink Lake Road. We turn there and proceed to the Trout Lake Road. We stop briefly at the Trout Lake Lodge and pick up some brochures, then return to camp to clean up, change clothes, and take a two hour nap. Then went into Bucks Midway Hardware Hank to check the moose kill registrations. We are the only license in our zone that is not filled. We are undaunted and a 100% confident that we will get our trophy. No big bulls have been registered, so they are still there for the taking and the Big Daddy is waiting for us.

Wednesday night is Burger Night at the American Legion in Grand Marais, and their burgers are good enough to warrant a break from hunting. It is great to take a ribbing and see old friends, and again we have the offers for help; "One call and there would be twenty guys calling in sick and covering every road and trail from the Brule River to the Canadian border. If we didn't get on the stick that might just happen all by its self." I thought, never doubt, we will have the last laugh. It is great having everyone, even strangers, checking on our progress and wishing us success in bagging a large trophy.

We can't help but rejoice among friends and enjoy delicious burgers, however, you guys in the Boundary Waters Canoe Area, we're sorry you have to cook hamburgers over an open fire after such a brutal day, and still have to gather firewood for tomorrow night, and get everything ready for morning before laying your tired bodies down on the hard ground. We don't envy you.

Day 6

Thursday, October 3

Moose, moose and more moose everywhere, and we still do not have our moose. We leave the bus at 4:45 A.M. and head up Highway# 61 to Hovland, then north on the Arrowhead Trail again. About two or three blocks on the right is the Old Settlers' Cemetery. This is the resting place for most of the first settlers to this remote wilderness and several markers date back to the very early 1800's. We will try to stop back here in the daylight if possible.

We again turn east on the Jackson Lake Road. Two miles in a large cow and her calf run out on the right side of the road. I hit the breaks and nearly stop. They run down the road on the incline, staying on the right side of the road as I follow about twenty yards behind them. The cow turns her head every few yards to be sure we are no threat to her calf. After about 500 yards, the cow ran into the woods and the calf followed. They are gone. These two are number five and six. The road from here on has many moose tracks and is really looking good. Also, a few timber wolf tracks are beginning to show up.

A few miles in on the left is the monument marking the trail to the site of the plane crash that took place on October 26, 1971. This crash claimed the lives of the pilot, Richard Ossanna, the guide, William Bushman, and Charles Carver, a sheriff from a southern Minnesota county, who had been on a fishing trip. The wreckage was finally discovered by surveyors on May 24, 1983, nearly twelve years later, while surveying for this very road.

The remains of the occupants were never found in this very remote area; however some of the crash and the scrap metal still remain on the hillside. The spot is marked by this monument placed there by the family of Charles Carver.

We again take stands on the Lake Andy Road, knowing that sooner or later we will have to see a moose, with all the tracks and fresh nipped saplings. After an hour and a half of watching the hillside where the most tracks had been the day before, no moose shows up and we return to the Otter Lake area. We want to check out the area on the landing over by Otter Lake again and go down the right hillside and check out that area, as there is a large amount of browse in that bunch of skid trails. I roll a large cedar cut off over to the edge of the landing and stood it on end for Megg to sit on. This will be a good vantage point, out of sight from the landing, but she can still see through the cover if anything shows up. This should be fairly comfortable, about four feet off the ground and some twenty-eight inches in diameter, and I will be able to see her from a wide area down below. I help her up onto it and she tries to get positioned so that she can see fairly well and that we will still be able to see each other.

My plan is to stalk the skid trails as quietly as possible and hope to get close enough to a big bull to fill our tag. There are five skid trails, really nice and straight, each about one fourth to one half mile long, although only one is in a position so I could see Megg. I told her to shoot one round in the air if she needs me for any reason and I will be here as fast as I can run.

I head down the hill. In about 200 yards the trails forked. Taking the first trail straight ahead so I could keep an eye on Megg (this is actually the second trail to the left). I now start stalking very slowly and walking on the balls of my feet. I am watching for any sound, movement, or variation in color and profile, paying particular attention to every evergreen. After about 150 yards of slow going and very rough walking, I notice a real dark shadow behind a small clump of evergreens. I froze. After what seems to be fifteen minutes or longer, there is a slight movement. It moves toward me a few feet, and I can see it is a big cow. She is feeding on fresh, young, tender aspen growth, and has not seen me. I slowly bend forward as far as possible with the gun cradled under my right arm along side my body and my left arm dangling straight down. I turn to my right and tip-toe quietly, sideways, and very slowly I proceed toward her.

At about forty yards she looks up and sees me. As she watches, I move ever so slowly toward her…just one soft, easy step at a time with left arm dangling, being ever so careful to step solidly on the balls of my feet without my heels touching the ground. This sounds like another animal walking. If the heel touches down, it makes a sound that is not normal in the wild, and will cause an automatic alarm. When I am about thirty yards from her, she steps out from behind the evergreens and takes a good look at me. Again I froze. The hair on the back of her neck is starting to rise. I start to back away and she lays her ears back. This is not good. I slowly back away as she watches intently. I remain in a leaving position so as not to startle her any further, but I am in a bad situation. I try to speed up my retreat as much as I can. After I have doubled the distance between us, she turns toward thicker cover and trots off. This is number seven. Wow, what an emotional surge… am I lucky to be off the hook! Usually when a moose lays his ears back, it means "fight!" and I'm definitely not a match for a charging moose, regardless of weapon size.

After this encounter I felt relieved and more confident as I move forward with extreme caution, about 200 yards down the trail, a big bull steps out to my left and trots down the road into the woods and out of sight. This is number 8; I had no chance for a shot.

Another 100 yards on my left is an area that is fairly open with a short open trail about fifty yards long and fairly open back the way I had just came from. Hoping to maybe see the cow again, I walk down about half way and step up on a large spruce that had broken off about six feet off the ground, yet was still firmly attached to the stump. There are several limbs that offered me steps to climb up on top and take a look around, and did I get a shock…in front of me about thirty yards and in the wide open space, watching me climb, was a yearling cow. Obviously, she is very curious. She has probably never seen a human being before; at least not one that climbs trees. She turns and trots off in the same direction as the other cow, this is number nine. This is really encouraging…five moose already today. Three in the last half hour…and I have stalked up on two of them. There are fresh moose tracks everywhere. This has to be one of their main feeding areas. The new growths of Aspen shoots are three to four feet high and have lots of leaves. All over there are patches that are nipped off about thirty inches off the ground. We **WILL** definitely, hunt this area. There is an ample food source for many moose in this large area of at least 200 acres. With its rapid growth, it is a renewable supply; plus there are patches of small evergreens and many skid trails that make walking easy for both animals and humans.

I return quickly to the main trail so I can see Megg again. She is farther than I had anticipated, about 450 yards away. I have left her alone and for a short while, out of my sight, something I had promised her I would not do. I hurried back to join her. We discuss my discovery and decide to go down the trail again and explore some of the other long straight tributaries reaching back closer to the standing timber. I help her down off her perch on the big cedar block and move it over about two feet where she felt it would give a better location for a full view.

We walk down the hill where the trails fork. There is a pile of cut off ends and tops that, once we are on top, gave us a good vantage point with a view down three trails and back up the hill to the cedar block that we had just left.

Megg climbs up on top of the cut off ends and gets positioned so we will be able to see each other. I proceed down the first trail exploring and looking for all signs of moose. This trail turns about 300 yards in, so I go back and looked over the other two remaining trails until they turn. One of these have a low wet spot with soft clay, imbedded with lots of different sized timber wolf tracks, as well as more moose tracks.

After I return, we sit on a spot that has a few large logs and eat our lunch. As we start back to the main landing, Megg notices her large cedar block is missing. I jokingly ask her what she did with it. She said someone must have come and removed it but she didn't see or hear anyone. I surmised she must have taken a nap while I was hunting the side trails. As we approach the landing, we see it behind some tops, somehow it has been tipped over and rolled, about twenty yards from where it was. We are both bewildered. As we get closer and can see on top of the landing, the whole area in an oval circle is all torn up. The area is about sixty by hundred feet and there is not a spot that has not been torn up. By the size of the tracks and the skid marks, there are three different bulls that really had it out. There are hoof and knee marks and horn gouges deep into the packed surface of the earth. Also, there are several gobs of black hair. This has to have been done while at least one of us was in full view, yet neither of us heard or saw anything. On the east side of the landing is a log pile of large birch waiting to be hauled. There are about forty cord of eight foot saw logs piled ten feet high and it is quite easy to climb to the top. An old skidder seat has been abandoned there, which made a good, solid seat for a stand. We place it on top of the pile facing the main landing to the north. Megg lays the guns down and climbs up to join me and to try it out for comfort and the best spot for the maximum area of coverage. I climb down, unload her rifle and hand it up to her to check and see if she can get positioned to use her knees as a rest for a steady shot. This is great, and will make a very good stand for this afternoon. I bellowed the female mating call as loud as I can in the three main directions twice from each position, then wait ten minutes and call again.

Since it is close to noon, we return to the bus. We let Cinnamon out on her thirty foot leash to get some fresh air and do her thing. We then set the alarm for 2:30 and take our daily nap. By now we are getting so tired we can go to sleep just by closing our eyes. It is necessary to get a nap each afternoon so we can stay awake and be alert on our stands. I am having trouble staying awake while driving back to camp at noon. When the alarm sounds, however, we jump up, load our gear and hit the road again.

We are now reaching the point of optimism and excitement is mounting with all the good signs in the areas that we are encountering after seeing five moose this morning; they are definitely starting to move. We arrive at our hunting site about 3:15 P.M. Due to the condition of the logging road, we decide to park at the edge of the landing and not go any farther or make anymore noise than absolutely necessary. I help Megg settle in on top of the log pile, then hand her the 30-06 Remington pump. She immediately and quietly loads it, checks the safety, and looks through the scope to make sure the lens is clean, then sets the Vari-power on 2 ½. I remind her to fire one in the air if she needs me for any reason. I will be just out of sight on the south edge of the landing, sitting on the large cedar block we placed earlier this morning. I load the 300 Weatherby Magnum and slip away as quietly as possible, returning to the big cedar cut off. I walk up on the two block steps I positioned earlier and sit down. Once comfortable, I vocally call the mating call two times, wait about five minutes, then call again.

Megg is northwest of me, and I can hear a lot of movement in the woods north of me, moving toward the west. By the position Megg is from me, I knew the commotion can not be made by her. I am positive it is at least two moose, maybe more. I call twice about every ten to fifteen minutes and then remain totally silent. I can hear a lot of slow movement going in a northwesterly direction. Whatever it is, it is trying to get downwind of me, and is moving ever closer to where Megg is. I call once more, wait for another twenty minutes. I am pretty sure I hear a real distant grunt, but can not be certain. I make a single quiet call and wait. I am not sure the moose are far enough into the rut for the call to be effective. For fear of over-calling, I decide to remain silent and wait. Boy is this cedar block getting hard and cold on the buns.

I slide over and step down on the blocks to get myself to the standing and moving mode. I have been debating starting to inch back towards the log pile, quite uneasy that Megg is alone. Ka-Pow! I am on the ground and running as fast as my cramped legs will allow. There is about a three second delay, then Bang-Bang-wham-bang-bang! I am now twenty yards up the slope and running. She has already emptied the clip. Megg is now in view trying to get another clip out of her parka pocket. She turns to look for me. I am already in full view and running, partly to get to her as fast as possible and to draw the attention away from Megg to myself.

One more step and I can see the back of a bull beyond the wood pile. Two more steps and I can see the whole animal and the back three quarters of another large moose, about 150 yards away.

"Which one are you shooting at?" I holler. She turns back and points in a forward direction. "Give me the direction," I yell.

She answers, "The left one, the one with horns."

This is confusing to me, since the right one had horns with about a forty inch spread. I did not dare shoot. If a person or party shoots two, you are facing a heavy fine and loss of hunting privileges for five years. Even wounding one of them would be an equal violation. So you must have signals to prevent this. Megg has never seen the horns on the one to the right. In her excitement, all she saw is the first and larger animal with big, heavy antlers, although they had come out together. The large antlers had held her attention.

With all the commotion, the moose starts running west. With the wood pile blocking my view, I am unable to shoot, regardless. To say the least, Megg is excited. She has seen her first moose while alone and actually in the outdoors, in the wild, plus it was a large bull with huge antlers. She had shot five times in rapid succession. This along with her excited condition had all the markings of a severe case of moose jitters (buck fever). These two make numbers ten and eleven. This whole situation is definitely my fault for not preparing her for the many details she will be confronted with. This is comparable to the opening morning blunder of non-preparation. The huge monster had stood, looking, and then walked across the road and out of sight. I should have briefed her on all situations and conditions and what to do should this condition arise. Now is a good time to instruct her while we wait a half hour before pursuing to see if we can find hair or blood.

Megg is one smart lady and a worthy hunting companion. She listened intently and actually lived each condition in her own mind, as if it was actually happening. She fully believes in me and trusts in my ability as a companion, woodsman and instructor. From this point on, she presents herself as a veteran, experienced hunter. Megg pushes me to my limit with solid questions in many areas of hunting that I have skipped or missed.

After twenty to thirty minutes and her second cigarette it is time to check for blood. She stays on the wood pile and directs me to the spot where the bull had been when she shot. While I am looking, I finally found a couple of tracks in the bark and sticks left by the skidder, but no blood. Finding no blood is not unusual for the first fifty to one hundred feet from the point of impact.

While roaming around in the brush looking for broken sticks and or blood, I jump a large cow (number twelve), which crosses the road we came in on. Megg got a good look at it, she knew exactly where it crossed and picked a spot in the woods to mark it, as we had talked about the importance of this earlier. The tracks are there and are easy to find. This cow may have been the reason the two bulls came out in the open. She jumps about 150 yards west of where the two bulls were.

I called Megg down to join me after she was sure where the bulls were when she shot, and I marked the spot. We look intently for blood and spread hooves for a sign of injury, but it is getting dark and it is very hard to see the marks with all the bark and leaves. We have to be exceptionally cautious and keep a watchful eye. It is clouding over and rapidly getting very dark. You do not want to get too close to 1200 to 1400 pounds of wounded bull in dense brush and slashings where you can hardly crawl, yet a moose can go through it like it is swamp grass. Megg's short legs are a real dilemma compared to my 6'2" height and long legs. I am getting crotch bound with nearly every step, trying to get through the jungle. Megg is down on all fours trying to get through each windrow, which are about fifty feet apart with a skid trail on each side. We soon decide it was too dark and dangerous to continue. We will return tomorrow morning at first light and resume the search.

It is a quarter mile from the landing to the car in total darkness, and it is very comforting to be in the wagon with the lights on and the heater on high. Volvos have a tremendous heating system, which sure feels good.

Megg at this time is very down emotionally, as anyone would be after failing. I know the feeling from back in 1988. With a lot of encouragement and kidding, too, she realizes that it is not the bitter end. We still have the best nine days left to hunt. The rut is now starting, we are seeing moose every place we go. Plus, the leaves are getting more colorful every day. By the time we reach the camper she was fine.

Day 7

Friday, October 4

Since we can't shoot anymore until we check out the previous day and it is raining hard off and on, we leave a little later than usual. Everything is soaked and sloppy wet. Within an hour we are soaked and miserable, yet we push on. We search everything within a quarter mile and even farther on the skid trails, looking as far as we can to see back in the woods. About 11:00 A.M., we became convinced it is a lost cause yet we drive the roads all around the area for another hour looking for moose and wolf tracks. If there is a wounded moose anywhere around, there will be wolves; especially since we have seen many fresh wolf tracks in this area.

The roads are getting sloppy from the rain, making it easier for wolf tracks to show up. But there are none. We give it up and return to camp to dry out, and to clean and oil the guns. We hang up our soaking wet clothes and change into dry ones, turning the heat up in the bus and opened four windows about an inch to let the steam out. We load the clothes we will need for the next three days, some food, and the dog's necessary items into the Volvo wagon. Put a note on the door and head down Highway# 61 to Lutsen and Caribou Highlands.

Friday, P.M.

CARIBOU HIGHLANDS

Megg has recently retired from Blandin Paper Company after about thirty-six years and her family gave her a retirement gift, a three day stay at Caribou Highlands executive condos at the base of Lutsen Ski Resort. This is definitely first class, and we are ready for some R&R. She left me with most of the work while she enjoys the pleasure of running water, a mirror and most of all, reacquainting her buns to a toilet seat. This is a treat; now for a nice hot shower and a quick nap. What a drastic difference from those souls braving the cold and rain in the remote areas of the Boundary Water Canoe Area. We have to remember to say another prayer for them tonight.

Dogs are not allowed in the condos, so I check with one of the guys outside and since I have no place to put Cinnamon he suggests we put down papers and a blanket and keep her by the storage closet, and we will be responsible for any damage. This is no problem because she is cleaner and more obedient than ninety-five percent of children. She peed in the woods and is so glad to be with us she curled up and went right to sleep. By the time I carry everything in and got things half-way organized, Megg had collapsed on the bed in the upper story master bedroom. I drop down beside her in total exhaustion for a quick moment of relaxation, before we go to the restaurant to eat. We are so exhausted from the long hours and hard miles of walking and fresh air, however that we slept on. Twenty hours later I am awakened by Cinnamon's bark tone saying, "I got to go **now**!" I run down stairs, untie her leash and heads for the woods on the run with her drizzling all the way. What a wonderful dog she is.

Day 8

Saturday, October 5

We are awakened at 1:00 P.M. by Cinnamon at Caribou Highlands. After her run in the woods it is back into the Volvo for her until I get her food and water out to her. She is absolutely starved and licked both bowls clean. Now it is my turn for a half hour soak in the hot shower to remove the fungus. My shower in the school bus consists of heating water on the gas kitchen stove, pouring it in a weed sprayer tank and pumping it through a hose to the shower head above the entry steps. It works great, but is very inconvenient when you spend all your time hunting. The porta-potti is likewise functional but inconvenient. This is a real treat to rediscover luxury with a toilet seat, TV, fireplace, microwave and a comfy bed…luxury beyond words. I say another quick prayer for those eager beavers twenty miles and two days back by canoe in the drowning rain. That takes guts and nerves of steel.

Megg knows the owners of Caribou Highlands, so we go over to the Bar & Restaurant for a couple of drinks and a big juicy steak. This is great and we still have two more days to relax and make plans for the most important part of our hunt. We go back to the condo, lite the fireplace and have a couple more drinks while watching the fire burn and watching cable TV. Soon we are drowsy, so we retire to bed fairly early.

Day 9

Sunday, October 6

Megg prepares a super nice breakfast for us: sausage, eggs, hash browns, English muffins, OJ and coffee; while I take Cinnamon for a ride out of the area and a walk in the woods. We relax for a while after breakfast, and then at 2:00 P.M. go over to watch the Twins game and have lunch at Papa Charlie's. After the game it is back to the condo to again relax as we watch the fire in the gorgeous fireplace.

My son, Terry, found my old beater Volvo wagon, and goes in to check on our success and invites us to come up to 9 Mile Lodge above Schroeder for a dinner and dancing starting at 7:30 P.M. The 9 Mile Lodge is a real scenic spot overlooking 9 Mile Lake with its varied green shorelines. We stay until 11:00 P.M. and get to see a lot of people we knew from the past. It is getting late and we don't care for rock music, so we head back to Caribou Highlands. What a waste for only two of us to use this beautiful place that is set up to accommodate 12-14 people without crowding. If we had only known a few days in advance, we could have had friends over for a party.

Day 10

Monday October 7

BACK TO BASE CAMP

After three days of mixed rain and heavy showers, the clouds break up and the forecast is for the sun to show up again today. We have had a good two days of relaxation and are again in high hopes of getting our trophy bull. After watching the news & weather on TV while the coffee perks, we get up just before 8:30 A.M. While Megg makes breakfast, I start packing up to check out. I take Cinnamon for a nice walk and fix her food. She is quite hungry and cleans up her dish. I tie her to the trailer hitch on the Volvo and proceed to carry out our suitcases and arrange the back end of the wagon.

There is only one other vehicle in the parking lot, parked about two stalls over. This is a very fancy Cadillac Baritz convertible with all the gold: grill, hub caps, mirrors and trim. I go in to have breakfast & coffee with Megg, who already has all the food packed and is ready to get going. We enjoy a leisurely breakfast and had our last cups of coffee. As I step outside with the large cooler, Cinnamon is going ballistic, growling and barking at the guy with the Cadillac Baritz. He is backed up against the door of the Baritz and looks as if he is about to be eaten alive. His golf bag is on the ground by his back door and he is desperately trying to get a club out. He is definitely something neither of us had seen before. He is dressed like he has just came from an audition for a part in the Lockharts or a Laurel and Hardy movie, wearing a pair of yellow and green plaid golfing knickers, bright yellow socks with the knickers tucked in, and a shiny green shirt partially covered by a yellow and green vest with diagonal print and a green and yellow plaid beret pulled forward. I could understand why Cinnamon was barking but I spoke to her and she stopped.

As I place the cooler in the wagon, I notice the golfer gentleman looking at our sad excuse for transportation. It is obvious he does not approve of my old beater with an inch of clay all around it. My left headlight is duct taped together and held in by a bungee cord and the grill is gone from colliding with an overgrown bambi about a month earlier. The gentleman has a very puzzled look on his face, to which I stated, "Yes, she might not look the greatest anymore, but she is still my deer killing, goose chasing, moose hunting buggy, and she has earned the right to be parked with the very best of the great ones."

He looks at me like I was crazy. Obviously, he is not impressed, so I wish him a good day and a great game of golf. I continue to load up. I don't think he has fully recovered yet. When I start bringing the guns out, panic must have hit again as he jumps into the Cadillac and takes off while still putting the top down. With all the wind pressure on it; it's amazing he did not tear it loose.

When I finish loading, Megg has cleaned and vacuumed the place so it looks wonderful again. We check out of luxury and head back to the wilderness where fun begins again. We decide to give it two more days, and then we will abandon the idea of a trophy and pick a nice one, regardless of antlers. Look out moose!! We are going for meat on Wednesday, but still hope for a sixty inch trophy.

As we drive up the hill from the parking lot toward the new exclusive condos, we take particular notice of the splendid colors on the hillside above us, a florescent display of nature. The trees are now changing to their full colors very rapidly, and we are about two days away from the peak of the season. We are again talking about the good fortune that brought us here. We have seen twelve moose in seven days. The rut is just starting and the big ones are now ready to start traveling. They will soon be moving through open clearings.

As we pull into Midway Service in Grand Marais, the registration station in our area, we are in need of gasoline again. After refueling, we check out the status and learn that no large bulls have been killed in the northeast section of our area, Zone 70. What's more, all other licenses in Zone 70 have been filled, and since our license is the only one remaining, we do not have to be concerned about other hunters killing "Our Trophy." We have never hunted the Powers Lake area and only two moose of no significance have been taken over there. If necessary, we may try it in a couple of days, once we start meat hunting. We may have a good chance of seeing a trophy bull before we shoot a nice cow. This seems very logical to us and all others who are aware of our situation.

After leaving Midway, we stop at South of the Border restaurant and pick up three California burgers to take out. We head east to the bus; our base camp. All of our wet clothes are now dry. It is really easy to unload and put everything in its place. We change into our hunting clothes and reorganize the Volvo to make our hunting easier as we move in and out with our gear and guns.

Since we decided to cruise the roads and look for tracks, we will take Cinnamon along. She has been left alone in the bus every time we went out hunting. The reasoning for this action is that this time of year the bulls are very aggressive. If Cinnamon were to see a moose close to the wagon she would go wild and the agitated moose would probably try to get at her and could very likely destroy the Volvo. Since we are just going to drive the roads, it will be fun to have her along; she can help look for wildlife.

Once more we drive up the beautiful North Shore to the Arrowhead Trail. The colors just explode under the clear blue sky in the bright sunlight. The farther we go, the brighter the colors become. The red maples are now showing. We turn right on Jackson Lake Road and drive about twenty miles per hour, taking in the beauty and looking for fresh tracks. We turn left onto Lake Andy Road and drive to the barricades at the cross trails, then return to the Jackson Lake Road until it intercepts the Swamp River Trail.

Because of the bright clear skies and the brilliant colors, we take a right and drive the extra mile to get some more pictures of the Pigeon River, and the interconnecting swamps in full color, from the Pigeon River heliport lookout. The Swamp River trail turns into Otter Lake road after we crossed Swamp River. The Otter Lake road is now in full color and absolutely fascinates both of us. Moose tracks are showing really distinctly on all of the roads after the weekend  drenching. We hit the Arrowhead trail, called the McFarland Lake Road years ago, from the upper end. Here we turn around and head back. As we pass Otter Lake, we make a last minute decision to park at the landing and walk in to the log pile and sit till dark.

THE RIGHT DECISION

We quietly let Cinnamon out for a few minutes while we get ready. I seriously warn her and emphasize she is not to bark, especially if she saw a moose. Once she is settled down, I quietly close the doors and locked them. We walk to the log pile where Megg had seen the two bulls and a cow, and had shot at the large bull. We also want to look at the soft ground for wolf tracks just in case she may have hit the one she shot at (before Buck Fever set in and she emptied the clip.). There are no wolf tracks, but there are fresh moose tracks everywhere. We stay together and both climb up on top of the log pile. In a couple of minutes we are somewhat comfortable and settle in for a long wait. I call two times about every fifteen minutes until the daylight starts to fade. It is about a half mile to the car so we start out while it is still light enough to watch our steps. I call again just as we leave the log pile and hear a loud crack against a tree out by the road. Within the last hour I thought I had heard this same reply in the far distance, but with the wind blowing I could not be certain. This sharp crack, I have been told, is a bull rapping his horns against a large tree to let the lonely cow know how large he is. He is on his way and to let other bulls know this is his territory and that he will fight to defend it. I had never heard this response to my calls before, so I am not totally convinced of what it is. Half way out, I call again and hear the same response, from the landing out by the road.

We reach the car at dusk, about 6:50 P.M. I immediately rearrange the wagon and lay the guns on the hood as we take off our parkas. I turn on the dome light to see better as we case the guns and make ready to head out. I had called the time and temperature number at the Duluth radio station for the correct time on the day prior to the season opening to be sure we had the exact time. For moose hunting in Minnesota, there is zero tolerance for mistakes and a heavy fine and loss of all hunting privileges for five or more years, depending on the exact offense.

Since it is getting dark, Megg asks: "What would you do if that big bull walked out right now?"

I glance at the clock on the dash and reply: "Within the next four minutes, I would drop him".

"You mean big like that evergreen over there? There is definitely a black spot in front of it." I am looking at the lights and back to the dark and back again and it is not easy to adjust that fast.

Excitedly, Megg says, "That's a moose with horns. Big ones!"

"Are they big enough to shoot?" I see the shadows. The bull has horns, all right, but my eyes can not adjust fast enough. I ask, "Are they big enough?"

"Yes, they are big."

Megg jerks the Remington out of the case as she hands me the butt end with the recoil pad across the hood in front of the windshield while stripping the case away. She is now halfway across the hood. She jerks the gun back and pops in the clip and I heard the click as it engaged. She jerks the action shut and says, "Shoot it."

Cinnamon is going ballistic when she sees me raise the gun to my shoulder. I can just imagine what is going through her mind, after being with me on numerous hunts and seeing many one-shot kills. She has seen quite a few moose over the years, and being that one of the characteristics of her breed is to be a herd dog, she would get excited, but nothing like this. In 1996, at about two years old, she had been savagely attacked by two wolves and would cower whenever she smelled them, so her action remains a mystery. However, it did cause the moose to look toward us and pause for a couple of essential seconds, giving us time to address Cinnamon's savage attitude. Her nocturnal eyes must have been able to see the timber wolf clearly, much more than we anticipated. It takes a second to settle her down and get her under control. I can only guess, that she surmised a one-shot kill would be lights out for her hated wolf, since she had seen me kill one of the two that attacked her in 1996.

A WELL PLACED SHOT

The scope is on four power, so the optics do not pick up enough light to give me a good shot, yet I can see the bull with a big black timber wolf right on his heals and a large cow and a calf about thirty feet out on the landing. I quickly lower the rifle and turn the scope to 1 ½ power. I forget about everything but the bull. Now I can see him clearly. I take a split second to be sure the cross hairs are exactly where I want them and squeeze the trigger. The muzzle blast is blinding so I can not see a thing. The K-thump took a lot longer to report than it should have. The solid hit is sure, and the range is farther than anticipated. In a split second's notice you do as you are told without question and that I did. I had previously made up my mind that Megg will be the one to shoot the moose. She is a very good shot, and with me by her side she will not miss again. I will back her up if necessary. She fells so bad about getting too excited and having missed her opportunity that she is reluctant to have it happen again. Furthermore, after hearing of my mistake fourteen years ago when I downed a beauty with approximately a sixty to seventy inch spread, then by being over confident and not following up to be sure he was dead, he got away and was never found. She was giving me another chance.

As the bullet impacted, Megg let out a yell. "You got him! I saw him go down. He really humped up when you hit him!"

I immediately unload the gun, case it and put it in the back seat luggage compartment. There is nothing in sight. There is no question in my mind that we have our moose, but where he may be when he finally dies, can be a different story. It is a little over a 150 yards, about twice the distance that it looked, and there lay our trophy. He had made one lunge on impact and dropped dead in his tracks with his rump on the landing. He fell with his head and horns on a mound that was pushed up when they had cleared the landing. His horns look enormous, and his size is definitely huge and very acceptable.

We stop and watch him for a couple of minutes to be sure he is dead, and not breathing. No need to push our luck any farther. Megg is absolutely on cloud nine and so happy for me that I am able to avenge my mistake of 14 years ago. There on the ground is exactly what we have came after, a big bull, shiny black and gorgeous, with large antlers. He looks like a big draft horse with horns.

There is little two people can do with an animal of this size in the dark. Our next move is to get help and get him in where he can be handled more easily. With timber wolves in the immediate area, time is critical. The time is now beyond the deadline for this day of hunting, as it is now 7:05 P.M. and pitch dark.

Getting help is no problem up here. Everyone who is a friend, sportsman, or acquaintance wants to get in on the action of helping when a large bull is bagged. We had at least twenty volunteers as soon as word was out that we had a license. We also had six who offered the use of their 4 X 4 ATV's. Although most were envious that we were drawn for a license, they are happy for us.

On the way back to Grand Marais to get help, we are very elated to have achieved our goal, although at this point we do not know how large our bull is or how his antlers will score by Boone and Crockett measurements. Now if we can just get him out and taken care of, as he should be, without timber wolf problems. When they hear the crack of the rifle and get a smell of fresh blood, to the wolves, this is the same as a dinner bell is to us. They are very familiar with the time essence of getting in for a free meal without the danger of getting a bullet in exchange. As we drive back, we again go over a list of the necessary things we have to do after we have this big monster in protective custody and away from the wolf packs. First is to get him hung up, dressed out, flushed out, washed as clean as fresh beef, and flooded with very cold spring water to lower his internal body temperature. Tomorrow morning we will have to call Taxidermy Unlimited and let them know we have our trophy. We will then get at the big task of skinning and capeing the neck up to his ears, packing the head with the cape attached and get it on top of the Volvo wagon for its long trip to Burnsville Minnesota, all in the same day.

GETTING HELP

Upon reaching Grand Marais, we drive right up to the front door of Bernekings, knock and enter. Dean is on the phone on a business call. He gestures, "Did you get one?" Both Megg and I, with big smiles, nod yes. Next he straightens out his available arm asking how large the antlers were. I point to the horns on the south wall below the vaulted ceiling and nod while stretching my arms out to about four feet.

Dean's whole expression changes. As soon as possible he ends the phone conversation. Then, with great enthusiasm and excitement, came the many questions:

"How big?

Yes, really big.

Size of spread?

Don't know for sure, Maybe 48.

Didn't you go up to it?

No.

Sure it's dead?

Oh yes, it is dead.

There is no blood on your hands!

No sense in trying to do anything alone in the dark.

Where is he at?

On the landing by Otter Lake;

Which one?

Boat landing or pulp landing?

Pulp landing…right on the edge of it, close to the road."

Dean's next reply is, "Good place; let's go get it." He put five gallons of gas in the pickup and put another five gallon can in the box to take along. He backs the pickup to his equipment trailer and hooks it up. Dean tells me to put everything we will need in the pickup box. I reply that I already have everything we could possible need in the back of my Volvo wagon that it will be a whole lot easier to drive both vehicles than to load just what we might need and have to unload and load again when we get back. And when we get there we might find that we need some of the equipment we left behind. Also, with the moose down and dead and wolves in the area, time is of the utmost importance before they start their feast.

When we arrive back at the scene, Megg gets right with the program. She handles the spotlight as if she has done it a hundred times before. It is really nice to have both vehicles to do the heavy work for us. We tie a one-half inch nylon rope to the horns and over the hook on the front of Dean's pickup, then tie another to the front leg and over to the trailer hitch on the Volvo. With Megg holding the light and watching what was happening, she directs both of us to ease the moose over on his back and spin him around so his horns, head, neck, and shoulders are on a small mound. This makes it much easier to open the stomach cavity and start removing the entrails to field dress it. Megg holds the light so I can see to turn the Volvo around and get the head lights on the whole moose. She handles that light like an old pro, which makes the job so much easier.

By now it is absolutely pitch black outside. Dean holds the back legs straight up and spread open and the gutting began. The 5/8" thick hide is still difficult to cut even with my razor sharp Buck fold-up knife. After dressing dozens of deer in my lifetime, I learned to go slow so as not to cut the paunch. Once the cavity is opened, the real hard work begins. I can only imagine the teams in the remote areas of the Boundary Waters Canoe Area trying to do this with a gas lantern in three or four feet of ice water. The intestines must weigh about 400 pounds, and there is about thirty gallons of blood that emptied into the chest cavity. I am 6' 2" tall and have long arms, yet I can not reach far enough into his chest cavity to cut the diaphragm all the way around to release the heart. It is all Dean and I can do to pull the huge pile of intestines from the cavity. After several attempts to cut the entire diaphragm loose from different angles, I have to give up and proceed with scooping the blood out of the intestinal cavity. We use the Volvo and ropes to flip him on his belly and drain the rest of the blood before loading him.

Dean turned the truck around and backed the equipment trailer up to the moose's head. Megg and I lifted the horns as hard as we could and could hardly get them off the ground so that Dean could get the trailer ramp started under the head. I used a ½" nylon rope to tie from his horns to a two-ton cable come-a-long. Next I place two six foot 2' X 12's under his head and up to the shoulders to form a skid to ease the pressure against the trailer ramps. This is done so we will not damage the hair around the neck and shoulders and spoil the appearance for mounting. The come-a-long is hooked to a tow chain around the trailer tongue. Dean starts pulling with the come-a-long while Megg and I pry on the horns and the 2' X 12' planks to get him started. An inch at a time, we get the head and horns up on the trailer.

Dean yells for us to get some more tackle on the moose because he is bending the handle on the come-a-long. We just can't believe how hard that dead weight is to move on rough, rocky terrain. I hook up a fence puller with a four gang pulley and 3/8" nylon rope to aid in the pulling. Megg and I pull with all the muscle we have to get it started and keep it moving. I am wondering if we are going to pull his horns off before we get him loaded. This is one big carcass and the trailer is full of moose. Leaving the come-a-long attached to his horns and tie to the trailer, we tie his back feet to the two sides to keep him from slipping or sliding. After picking up the site and shining the million candle power spotlight over the area to be sure we have loaded everything, we head for town.

Dressing and loading took three of us just under two hours. This is the way an old timer learns by his years of mistakes; to shoot one right on the landing on hard level ground, with power equipment waiting. What a difference from doing a job like this up in the Boundary Waters Canoe Area by brute force. Compare this with what those guys are doing to handle their trophy moose. If you can just imagine working by a gas or kerosene lantern after midnight in four feet of icy water, trying to handle upwards of 1400 pounds of dead weight. Being exhausted, cold and hungry, and having to keep going until that animal is taken care of. The meat must be guarded from bear and wolves.

It must also be packed into coolers to prevent spoilage. This is generally done in the dark by dim light in the worst of conditions. I'll bet most of these guys regret ever getting involved in moose hunting. I know quite a few who went this route with not even the slightest inkling of what they were getting into. Then they still have to get their moose and all their gear back to civilization in forty-eight hours. Everything must be cleaned up. All burnable items must be burned; all other items must be taken out with you. The fire pit must be totally burned and the fire out prior to leaving.

Our situation is very different. As we arrive back at Berneking's,

Dean starts up the big John Deere loader. We get a small logging chain over the bucket and hook it to the nylon ropes. Very easy, with no effort, up comes the moose. As Dean runs the bucket, I drive the trailer out from under the moose. Dean cut a board to hold the cavity open as I hook up a hose to his shop hydrant and start hosing down the moose from the inside to cool the meat and wash out the bloody cavity. Then Megg takes over the washing job while I help Dean unhook the big trailer and put everything back where it belongs. Dean is exhausted from a real hard day and the long hours he works plus the great job he did helping us. Words can not express the deep appreciation we have for all of their help.

Megg snuck off and went to bed while I take over the washing and cooling of the whole carcass for another two hours. Berneking's deep well extends into an ice cold spring so the water is super cold and has extremely high pressures. This is a real plus, and very handy for cooling the meat as soon as possible. This will give us many hours of safety cushion for the time it takes to skin and process the meat. After two hours of this, I head for bed and the warm comfort of the bus. It has been one long, exhausting, but a very happy day. We have our trophy and it is secured.

Cinnamon is now happy and content to have us together in the bus. She has to be right beside us and watch over us all through the whole process with the moose. She has to be sure that big animal with those big horns didn't get after us. Her savage attitude when we first saw it more than likely caused it to stop for a second look, giving us that extra second for a clear shot and a clean kill.

Tuesday, October 8

Day 11 6:00 A.M.

Dean is already up and moving equipment before I make it out to check on the moose. I can now take a good look at our trophy. He is magnificent! His horns (antlers) are very even, dark walnut colored with the three long, heavy foreword points on either side are polished clean. His beautiful thick coat is unblemished and glistening black, in perfect prime condition. We are getting ready to drop it on the trailer again and take it in to Midway Service to register it. Just by chance, one of the employees at Midway who inspects moose stopped in to see Dean. He inspected the moose and okay'd it for us to skin it and to take the head and cape in for them to extract a portion of the lower jaw. This is supplied to the Department of Natural Resources for them to inspect and test for age and health conditions. (It is 4 ½ years old and in excellent health.) We lower it down about four or five feet so I can finish dressing out the heart and lung diaphragm. This is quite simple, since it was washed clean the night before.

Upon close inspection, the 220 grain Round Nose Hornandy hand load had passed through the top of the heart. It had hit a rib, expanding it, so it did a super job of severing all of the arteries from the heart. This had eliminated all blood pressure so there is no bloodshot tissue at all. What luck!! No mess to clean up in the chest. There is only about a cup of bloodshot tissue on each side where the bullet passed through the muscle and flesh. It is very easy to trim and clean, compared to the normal amount of waste from a shoulder injury. However, it is rare for the bullet to exit through the hide on the opposite side because the 5/8" thickness is extremely tough. It will pull loose and act as a stopping shield but will not exit. The bullet is lying just under the hide.

We lower it down and re-hook the hind legs with a gambrel bar and start raising it. With this much weight on the head and horns against concrete, it is likely we will break or damage the tines, so we take precautions and pad the concrete with heavy cardboard covered with an old poly tarp. This prevents breaking any of the points.

Because of the bulk of the chest, even though it is washed well, some of the waste tissue remains and this has to be removed quickly to prevent spoilage. The carcass has to be skinned from the hind quarters down the belly to the front legs and then cut off. Then it must be cut very straight and evenly up the center of the back to the antlers, being careful not to cut the ears.

With the height of the hoist and the tilt of the bucket, it is just high enough to get the horns off the concrete apron. The cardboard keeps the points safe from breakage, even with the heavy weight of the moose on them while it is raised and lowered for skinning and cleaning. I start skinning the hind legs at 6:30A.M., going as fast as I can and being careful not to damage that beautiful hide. As the hide drops down over the rump, it is surprising to find that the rump is still body-warm. Still it is understandable, since the hide is 5/8 of an inch thick and the hair of the winter coat is very dense and hollow. The outside temperature is on forty-eight degrees, so the meat cools naturally. As the hide is cut loose, its own weight pulls it down, making it easy to remove. By 8:30 A.M. (two hours later), it is skinned down to the front legs. It is marked and cut off at that point.

At 8:45 Megg has breakfast ready and I have the back split up to the ears. While having breakfast and coffee, Megg reminds me to call Marv Gaston at Taxidermy Unlimited. Marv is happy for us, but surprised to hear that we have succeeded in getting our trophy. He advised that unless I am experienced in skinning out the head for mounting, I would be wise to have them do this part of the skinning. It is a very intricate job of cutting the skin free around the ears, eyes, nostrils, and mouth, and the correct procedure is absolutely essential. Just one slip and the damage will be almost impossible to repair. Megg and I have already decided to have them take care of this part of the process. We have our trophy, so why take a chance on damaging it. Marv passes the phone to Betty, his lady friend, and she gave me their cell phone numbers. She said they will be available to open at any hour that we brought it in. The phone is now passed to one of their team who gives me instructions on how to prep the hide and keep it cold and dry. He tells me not to use salt and to get it to them the following day.

After breakfast and coffee, I continue to skin out the front half. I split the hide at the front legs and skin them out to the knees and remove the fore legs and feet from the carcass. As I remove the hide from over the hump, I am amazed to find the body temperature is as warm as if it has just been killed. It was still as warm as the back and rump were two hours earlier. Furthermore, the whole carcass was hosed down for two hours last night with ice cold water. The 5/8 to 3/4 inch thick hide with the winter coat of hair is an incredible insulation against the cold. This is why it is a must to get the hide off as soon as possible and get it to start cooling to prevent spoilage. The temperature is dropping to about forty-eight degrees at night and only rising to about fifty-four degrees by mid-afternoon...a perfect temperature for curing. Because of the bulk of the chest, even though it is washed well, some of the waste tissue remains. Time is important to remove all contamination to prevent spoilage. The cape has to be split down the back clean to the ears and antlers for mounting. After skinning it down to the ears, I remove the head with the hide attached. I use Dean's Milwaukee Sawzall with a long blade, and this workes perfectly for cutting through the neck. Megg helps me wash off the trailer and we put the antlers, head and cape on it. It is now just noon. The outside temperature has only climbed to fifty-two degrees with the cold air blowing in off Lake Superior.

THE REGISTRATION

We haul the trailer with its precious cargo in to Buck's Midway Service, the official registration station. It is such a beautiful rack with its even symmetrical antlers that Scotty at Midway asks us to wait; while he runs across the street to the Cook County News for them to come and get pictures for the paper. At this point we did not have the time to notice the very even symmetrical configuration of the antlers with three even heavy points on each side of the forward panels. Its shinny jet black hide is beautiful and perfect. We are immediately swarmed by people and cameras flash. With a trophy like this, we are celebrities. Everyone has questions and many of them.

Because of the trailer, the only place we can park is on the highway side in front of (S.O.B.) South of the Border. This draws another crowd. Peggy, the waitress, took our orders just before their 2:00 P.M. closing time. Jimmy, the owner, being an avid sportsman himself, stays open a few minutes longer so we can eat. He also is a super nice person. Word passes quickly and we have heavy traffic from local people and grouse hunters that afternoon. Many are very surprised to hear this is the fifteenth moose we had seen, with the cow and calf being number thirteen and fourteen. Cook County News did a really nice article including a picture of us with the head and cape on the trailer.

Marge Helmer of Grand Rapids and Loren Bartels of Swatara, Minnesota had a successful Moose hunt. They bagged this large male with a 306. It has a 44-inch antler spread

Photo by Deidre Kettunen

71

As soon as possible, we return to camp. We spread the hide and cape out on the shop floor to cool and dry slightly. I again call Taxidermy Unlimited and tell them we will be bringing it down tomorrow afternoon, along with the front legs and feet to have a gun rack made. They did not want any of it salted if we can keep it cool until we deliver it to them. The cold wind blowing in across Lake Superior will cool it even more as we drive along the shoreline for 110 miles.

The next operation is to split the brisket, or sternum, and the groin bones and dress it completely, including removing the esophagus and trimming the diaphragm. As briefly mentioned before; while removing the heart, I confirm how perfectly the shot was placed. The bullet sheared off all the valves on the heart. This eliminated the blood pressure and kept the blood from flowing between the plies of muscle along the shoulder and rib cages. There is only about a cup of damaged meat on both sides from the bullet. There is only one bullet hole in the hide where the 220 grain Hornandy entered and on the other side the hide was pulled loose in a large area but it had stopped the expanded bullet and no damage was done to the hide on that side. The hide was perfect with no cuts or scrapes to indicate he had been fighting. This old boy must have been a sissy, because he has no marks on his head or hide. His heavy, dark antlers are nearly perfect, with no broken tines; unlike the bull fourteen years ago that had three broken ribs and a punctured lung, one eye recently gouged out, his scull cap pealed back about four inches, and one nostril torn way back. He had cuts and scars all over his head and shoulders.

Also, he had healed scars that had cut through the thick hide the full length of his body which had been made by a very large bear. Or very likely, he had escaped from a bear attack when he was a calf, and quite possibly the mother had fought the bear off. One horn had been broken nearly off when it was still in the velvet. It had healed crooked, but was completely intact. Also, he had started to charge when the two brothers, Doug and Don cut him down. This moose had been a real fighter.

Our next chore is to hose the inside of the carcass with cold water again to remove any contaminates and to check the outside for hair. Late in the afternoon, I inserted a one and a half inch piece of PVC pipe about four inches long into the bottom and top for air ventilation and wrapped the entire carcass in new .06 mil clear poly. He is now ready to cure for two days. The forecast is for temperatures to range from forty-six degrees to fifty-four degrees, perfect for curing. These two days will allow us time to take the head down to Burnsville to be mounted and the meat will cure nicely while we are gone.

We make several phone calls to let our family and friends know we will be coming down with the head and cape so they can see it before we take it to the taxidermist. I also call members of the Moose Willow Sportsmen's Club to tell them we will be stopping briefly at the Corner Club in Hay Point if they want to take a look. Once we have everything organized and ready for tomorrow's trip, it is time for a short well deserved rest.

We wash up, and go into Grand Marais to the Legion Club for their $1.00 Burger night. We soon found out that Tuesday night is also "trivia night." Two people can play as a team and you pick your team name. We didn't have any idea what to use for a name, so Scotty (the person who registered our moose, is emcee for the trivia), starts calling us the "Moose Hunters." When a question is given, each team writes down their answer and takes it up to the table. When everyone has turned in their answers, they are read out loud and everyone gets a laugh. The right answer is given, and those who have it correct receive points. At the end of the evening the team with the most points wins a cash prize. The last place team wins a bag of cheese puffs for being full of hot air.

At the half time break, we request a name change from "Moose Hunters" to "Dumb and Dumber." Scotty announces it and everybody gets a big laugh. It is a wise choice, because we take last place and get the cheese puffs.

This is a fun group and we had a very memorable time. After big, delicious burgers, fries, and a couple of drinks, we leave early. Tomorrow we will have a busy day, with a lot of miles and a lot of stops. Again, after getting a bellyful of good food and being among so many good friends, I am thankful for our good fortune and progress. Compare this to what it would be, at this time of the hunt, if we are up in the remote areas of the Boundary Waters Canoe Area. If luck is with them, they are probably trying to protect their meat from wolves, and bears. They now have to start packing for a long two days of getting everything out while racing against time to keep the meat fresh. They will more than likely have to contend with bear and timber wolves following them out and trying to get into the coolers during the night. Here pepper spray and ammonia are a must to discourage intruders.

Day 12

Wednesday, Oct. 9, 6:00 A.M.

THE TRIP TO THE TAXIDERMIST

Rain is forecast for farther south, so the head and cape must be protected. This however, will be good for keeping it cool. We tightly wrap and tie the head and cape with light rope. We then cover it with heavy .06 mil poly and use "good old duct tape" to secure it. We tape it tightly around the antlers to prevent the water from getting in. Because the John Deere is being used with the moose hanging from the bucket, we have to build a platform to get the head and cape on top of the Volvo. It is all Megg, Marietta and I can do. The weight of it put a big dent in the top of the wagon. The dent stays there for several weeks before I am able to pop it back out again. Once loaded and tied down, the antlers look massive on top of the wagon.

We again stop at S.O.B. (South of the Border) for breakfast. About half of the cars that went by, slowed down and many pulled over to stop and take a good look. Cameras flashed continually. Again, we are instant 'back woods celebrities.' After eating we have to excuse ourselves from the well wishers and head out to get gassed up at Holiday, show our friends there our trophy and get on the road.

About every third car or truck coming toward us on the highway gives us a beep-beep and thumbs up. Others that pass us will pull along side and wave before passing. Some even roll their window down and want to talk. I did not want to be rude but this is not a good practice on a narrow, hilly and crooked highway at fifty-plus miles per hour, so we just wave and keep going. Obviously, people as a whole are pleased and make us feel special. A couple of naturalists did shake their fist at us, but it takes all kinds. The beautiful fall colors are now progressing daily as they move towards their fall splendor. Their awesome movement dancing in the variable winds creates a picture of elegance. This is truly a special day in our lives. When we stop in Floodwood for gas that will last until we reach the Twin Cities, we have a cold soft drink, as we usually do on our way to Grand Rapids. Here I get a brief lesson from a lady about wildlife preservation. I do respect everyone's opinion so I listened to her side of the Isack Walton issues against killing fur bearing animals. Though I elaborated on the life span of animals in the wild and the wasting of their furs and meat by not being harvested in a timely manner, plus the quick kill of a rifle compared to being savagely being torn apart and partially eaten alive by wolves and bear. She is not any more convinced with my side of the issue than I am with hers, so we excused ourselves and we get on the road again.

Since many people in the Grand Rapids area knew we had been drawn for a moose license, we thought it would be appropriate to let our friends know the outcome of our hunt. Our first stop is the Grand Rapids Herald Review office. They are very pleased with our success and want pictures of the moose horns on top of the wagon with us admiring our trophy. It will be published in the Sports section of the paper with a short write-up.

The next stop is Glen's Army Navy Store, where we had purchased some of our hunting supplies and the hat "For our Decoy." We just have to do a little bragging to our good friend Rusty Eichorn, who is also a member of the Moose Willow Sportsmen's Club. Rusty is an avid hunter and shoots trap at our gun range, also I might add, he is a very good shot. To our disappointment, Rusty is not in, so we leave a message for him and invite the staff at Glen's to take a look at our trophy. They are thrilled for us. Within minutes, a crowd gathers.

Our next stop is Megg's workplace at Central Square Mall. Her co-workers take turns coming out to look at the size of the antlers. Outside in the parking lot, a crowd is gathering again and since a few know

Megg, she is now the center of attention, second only to the moose. What a feeling of accomplishment we have along with pride and joy for succeeding in bagging a fine trophy. We stop briefly at Megg's home to call the Corner Club at Hay Point to inform them that we will be there in a half hour, since it is right on our way to Burnsville. After a short stop, we are on our way again, and three hours or so later approach the Twin Cities. Since Megg's daughter and her husband live in Lakeville, we decide to swing by their home and show them our trophy. They are very impressed. Her son-in-law is really thrilled, because he had loaned Megg his 300 Weatherby Magnum for the hunt. From here we call Taxidermy Unlimited to let them know we will be at their shop within the hour.

Betty is waiting with real enthusiasm to open up for us, even though it is after hours. She took possession of the head, cape, horns, front legs, and hide. This is a big mistake when I give them the rest of the hide instead of having it tanned, since it has such a beautiful unblemished black fur. While there, we have a chance to look at some of their other mounts, all beautifully done. The ones of special interest to us are the cougar on a ledge, the full body mount of a bull moose, a very large grizzly standing on his hind legs, a beautiful white, mountain  goat, and a huge alligator. They all look so alive it is almost fearsome. Obviously, we have truly made the best choice in our taxidermist.

By now it is after 9:00 P.M. with only one stop for gas and a burger to eat on the way, we head back to Grand Rapids. We arrive at Megg's after midnight and retire immediately. This has been a long day, and we have driven just under 600 miles and made all those stops.

Day 13

Thursday, Oct. 10, 6:00 A.M.

Once again, I am up early, put the coffee on, took a shower and awakened Megg. She has to have coffee before her shower, but that is okay; it gives me time to bring in the gear that we are finished with. I am very concerned about the temperature and the forecast, and fell that we definitely need to get back to Grand Marais. We need to plug in the freezer mounted on the trailer, so it has time to cool down in preparation for the moose meat.

I take the time to stop at Cub to buy a full roll of heavy wrapping paper, two rolls of tape, and two magic markers. When I return, Megg has taken her shower and is doing her hair, so I return a few calls that are on the answering machine. One is from my son Terry. He is coming up to Grand Marais this coming weekend, and we would like for him to pick up the antlers at Taxidermy Unlimited and bring them up with him. He is presently working close to Burnsville, and agreed to swing by and pick them up. I then call Taxidermy Unlimited and authorize him to pick them up, and for them to release the antlers to him. They told me the head would be skinned out late that afternoon and he could pick the antlers up between 4:00 P.M. and 5:00 P.M. If necessary, they would have someone there later, if he called them and gave them the specific time he would be there. They have been so helpful and cooperative.

We load a few more supplies that will be beneficial for processing: large heavy plastic bags, twisties, and my seasonings for making sausage, brats, polish, and beer sticks. I prefer Hamms Seasonings that are blended in Anoka, Minnesota. We again stop at Cub Foods and buy some fruit and miscellaneous groceries for next week's food supply while we process the moose meat. We start out again, heading East on Highway #2 towards Proctor. We make our usual stop at Starvin Marvins for breakfast. The landscape along Highway #2 is now brilliant yellow and red, with patches of evergreens lending a random contrast. It is warmer here than further north, so by the time we get to Grand Marais, the North Shore with its gorgeous colors will have reached its peak. Soon the beauty takes our minds off the work we have waiting for us. We look forward to the view from Spirit Mountain across the St. Louis River to the hills on the Wisconsin side. They will now be aglow with colors. As we approach, we find that they are even brighter than we had imagined.

DULUTH IS A FISHING PORT FOR LAKE TROUT AND SALMON

The blue waters of Lake Superior are rippling in the light breeze as many smaller fishing vessels congregate while trolling with artificial lures over schools of lake trout and salmon. This is a very popular activity this time of the year for sport fishermen, since the sea lampreys have been nearly eliminated. The lamprey is a parasite of large dimension up to sixteen inches long. They have a suction-cup shaped mouth that attacks the trout and attaches to the skin by suction. Small teeth within the center of the suction-cup continually grind through the soft scales so the blood can be sucked out of the trout. Several lamprey may attach to the same trout, weakening it and causing its death. When the lamprey's hunger is satisfied, they will release it, and when hungry again, will attach to another trout. The lake trout have made a remarkable recovery. At one time, the lake trout were in serious danger from the sea lamprey, which came in on ocean-going vessels through the Great Lakes and adapted to fresh water. They multiplied rapidly and nearly killed off the trout. As the lamprey multiplied and the lake trout population declined, one would find larger trout with several scars, some healed and some fresh. The trout would survive until it became too weak from loss of blood to catch its own food and eventually would die. The dead bodies would wash ashore and provide food for seagulls, eagles, and other birds of prey. Through combined efforts of state and federal agencies, a method of electric shock was developed, and used along with chemicals, to control reproduction of the lamprey.

As we enter Duluth, we see that the hills on the north side up along the Skyline Drive are nearing their full colors of yellow, orange, red, pink and brown. The Enger tower still stands proud and tall like a watchful sentinel towards the east end of the drive, it has been a fascinating landmark for over a century. It is a reminder of the early history of this magnificent port.

Every trip through Duluth is exciting. There are so many interesting structures of the past and present. The huge modern DECC is a beautifully designed structure used for conventions, large performances, etc. The William A. Irvin floats at the dock. The Irvin has been retired after serving the Great

Lakes shipping industry for many years, and is now a tourist attraction for the public to tour.

After passing through the scenic tunnels and continuing east we pass in front of many beautifully preserved mansions of the early shipping merchants. We next pass the front of the high wire security fence that helps isolate the massive Congdon Mansion. Beside it is the large parking lot for those wishing to tour this historic building. The buildings alone cover several acres.

There is so much to see along both sides of Highway #61 as we proceed through Duluth again and out of traffic congestion along the lake shore with its beautiful colors and sparkling blue waters rippling in the sun. Time goes by all too quickly as we take in the astonishing scenery of the many waterfalls and rivers that make up the beauty of the North  Shore Drive. Soon we top the hill, and below us is the picturesque stone wall that protects the town of Grand Marais from the violent storms. (The street and businesses along the waterfront were destroyed a few years ago making this barrier very necessary.) This harbor is still unique with shops and fish houses, many still operated by the descendants of the original families.

We by-pass everything to go directly to the bus, plug in the freezer and check out the moose. The moose is curing perfectly and is ready for processing. Dean and Marrietta have the meat processing room all ready for us to use. I unload the wrapping supplies and our food items, and we have a quick lunch, as we are both anxious to get started with the processing. The moose is hanging by the hind legs from the loader, and measurements are taken. From the actual usable meat on the hind legs to the end of the neck, it is eight feet four inches. The remaining neck is twenty-two inches long and twenty inches in diameter where the head was removed. I place two heavy saw horses with a plank deck covered with poly and wrapping paper under the neck to help catch the heavy sections. The neck is removed in two pieces with the aid of a long blade Sawzall. The two inch outside layer is removed for grinding and the large sections are placed into heavy plastic bags, vacuum sealed, wrapped and put in the bottom section of the freezer. We are now able to lower the carcass so I can remove the tenderloins and the back straps. The back straps are left out to be sliced and wrapped first. The tenderloins will be tonight's dinner for us and the Bernekings. A feast fit for a king. The moose is now split down the back as the quarters are removed and dropped on the platform. The carcass is lowered as I go for easy separation. Each section is placed in a large white bag, marked and frozen, to be re-thawed and cut up as time permits. The rump and part of the back are left out to be cut and wrapped in meal-size-packages. Each portion is vacuumed in plastic, sealed, wrapped in freezer paper, marked, and frozen.

Day 13

Friday, Oct 11

The thawing process is taking longer than I expected, giving us time to take a nice drive up to where we shot the moose. There is not a trace left by the wolves. It is like nothing had ever happened here. The blood is even licked clean from the rocks and soil. When we return to the bus, Terry is here with the antlers which he had stopped at Taxidermy Unlimited and picked up for us. They have been green scored at forty-five plus inches and beyond 170 inches in point score. Above all, they are symmetrical, nearly perfect, with only a one inch difference between the two sides.

Dean and Marietta are here every spare minute helping us cut and wrap; showing us the proper way to section and cut the meat. They give us full permission to use their steak tenderizer, grinder, saws, knives, and meat utensils. They are very cautious who they allow to use their equipment. They know I am extremely careful in the use, care and cleaning of the facilities. They have a lifetime of experience in meat processing and really know the best and easiest way to do things. Without their help, we would have been lost.

There is a huge difference between a monster of this size and even a large deer. As we start to cut one section, another is set out to thaw. All grinding meat is put into heavy bags and frozen for later preparation. These will be thawed all at one time, to be ground, seasoned with various seasonings for the various delicious brats, summer sausage, breakfast sausage, salami, wieners, and beer sticks. All will be ready for my smoke house, where sugar maple chips are used for smoking to give the meat a savory, tasty, distinct, flavor. The smoke house is the remains of a ten foot refridgerator, which I converted to a smoker. It has twelve slides, two and three quarters and three inches apart, for shelves of steel grates. They may be all removed to allow for hanging tubes of various sausages to be cured and smoked. It is heated by electric coils which also heat the wood turning it to charcoal and creating a smoked flavor. Various wood chips of maple, apple, mesquite, cherry, hickory or alder are used for various meats and fish to obtain many choice flavors.

Day 14

Saturday, Oct. 12

This processing lasts several more days. There are many short breaks to light a burner under the fry pan, add a little oil, and sample our progress and our expertise in seasoning. Dean has many large deep stainless trays for sorting and mixing at our disposal. The curious friends that stop in really enjoy the sampling, and their visits also give us bragging time about picking out and shooting only the nice, tender moose. The meat has been cured perfectly and most cuts are really tender. It is all very delicious. Still, it is a welcome break in the work to bring Megg back to Grand Rapids, to get back to her job. This is far beyond the three days her family gave her, before she would be calling one of them to help get her out of this backwoods ordeal.

Day 15

Sunday, Oct. 13

Before leaving we take a loop up around our hunting area. The leaves have now all fallen, and we run into snow squalls, making visibility almost zero. Fortunately this is a small belt of bad weather that cleared as we get back to Highway #61. As we leave Grand Marais, Megg became very quiet and I notice tears in her eyes as she realized this exceptional, wonderful trip is drawing to an end. She became very sad and remorseful, and I also felt very remorseful, but am pacified and comforted knowing that we will  soon have a beautiful mount to remind us of the highlight of our life together. My son, Terry later had a commercial artist do a composite picture of our highlights during the ten days we hunted. This was burned into a two and a half inch diagonal cut of white pine and permanently sealed in clear epoxy. This is a gorgeous piece of art. Terry is a super hunter and outdoorsman, yet he is a warm hearted individual who never forgets to show his love and appreciation for the years we have enjoyed the outdoors together.

Day 16 – 18

Monday – Wednesday

I return to Grand Marais, finish the processing, cleaned up the facilities, hooked up the trailer with the freezer on it and cleaned the school bus. I left one third of the best cuts in Berneking's freezer as a thank you, for the use of their facilities and for all their help. They are wonderful, talented people with hearts of gold. After saying many thank you's and farewells, I was on my way home.

In January, Megg threw a big seventieth birthday party for me at the Corner Club and invited our friends and Sportsmen's Club associates. Moose stew and moose brat burgers are served to all who stopped by, a perfect climax to my lifelong ambition of bagging a trophy; **"THAT EVEN THE VERY RICH CAN ONLY DREAM OF!"**

The taxidermist said that this was the nicest set of antlers he has ever mounted. Also, it was the nicest job of skinning he has ever had in the shop. I have done a lot of skinning throughout my lifetime. As a young boy I trapped and snared, doing all my own skinning. From age thirteen until now, I have skinned many dozens of deer, so I am quite experienced. However, I was exceptionally careful with this lifetime trophy, but, was still very pleased to hear this. Now as people stop by to see the antlers and ask questions, we take the time to chat for a few minutes. It was fairly well known that we were after a trophy. Although most doubted we would succeed, they were still elated that we had achieved our goal. All three news papers, the Cook County News, the Grand Rapids Herald Review, and the Aitkin Age, each took our picture and did a write-up in the sports sections.

For a few days we are sports celebrities and enjoyed every minute of it. This was really fun while it lasted, and it will be remembered for the rest of my life…the pride of accomplishment. The antlers were displayed at the Minnesota Deer Hunters Classic at the St. Paul Coliseum in February of 2003. The rack drew a lot of attention because of its uniform, even antlers and the symmetrical configuration. It was scored 173 and 6/8 with just over a forty-five inch spread. It lost a lot of width due to the symmetrical configuration, but it is, indeed, unique. It is now displayed at the Loyal Order of Moose #2023 in Grand Rapids, Minnesota.

Two words say it best:

MISSION ACCOMPLISHED

I have preached from the pulpit,
I have sang in the choir,
I have looked down on the Saint,
And looked up to the lair,

I have walked tall in the sunshine,
Crawled alone in the dark,
I've stolen love from my loved ones,
Like a thief in the park,

I've tracked wolves in the forest,
Lived on meat from the plains,
I've been lost in the wilderness,
And was cleansed by the rains,

I've caught fish from the river,
I've netted smelt from the lake,
I've saved the life of a frog,
By killing the snake,

I've pulled bullets from my flesh,
Had life pulled from my veins,
I've been thrown from a horse,
My wrist locked on the reins,

I've seen the tornado dip down
Crushing man with its tail,
I've seen the path through the forest,
Stripped clean by the hail,

I've seen blizzards rage on,
I've seen the fire destroy,
I've seen man at God's mercy,
Like a discarded toy,

I've been carved by the scalpel,
I've been robbed by a friend,
I've had a wife and a girlfriend…
Both used me to the end,

I've drank whiskey from the keg,
I've chased women by the score,
I've given the world a taste of heartache,
And I've received a lot more,

I've labored till I've dropped,
I've worked years for this pain,
But I would gladly give it all,
To once again,
Be cleansed by the rain.

Loren J. Bartels